ADVANCED IQ TESTS

The toughest practice questions to
test your lateral thinking, problem
solving and reasoning skills

PHILIP CARTER

KOGAN PAGE

London and Philadelphia

Publisher's note

Every possible effort has been made to ensure that the information contained in this book is accurate at the time of going to press, and the publishers and author cannot accept responsibility for any errors or omissions, however caused. No responsibility for loss or damage occasioned to any person acting, or refraining from action, as a result of the material in this publication can be accepted by the editor, the publisher or the author.

> Whilst the author has made every effort to ensure that the content of this book is accurate, please note that occasional errors can occur in books of this kind. If you suspect that an error has been made in any of the tests included in this book, please inform the publishers at the address printed below so that it can be corrected at the next reprint.

First published in Great Britain and the United States in 2008 by Kogan Page Limited

120 Pentonville Road	525 South 4th Street, #241
London N1 9JN	Philadelphia PA 19147
United Kingdom	USA
www.koganpage.com	

© Philip Carter, 2008

The right of Philip Carter to be identified as the author of this work has been asserted by him in accordance with the Copyright, Designs and Patents Act 1988.

ISBN 978 0 7494 5232 2

British Library Cataloguing-in-Publication Data

A CIP record for this book is available from the British Library.

Library of Congress Cataloging-in-Publication Data

Carter, Philip J.
    Advanced IQ tests : the toughest practice questions to test your lateral thinking, problem solving, and reasoning skills / Philip Carter.
        p. cm.
    ISBN 978-0-7494-5232-2
    1. Intelligence tests. 2. Self-evaluation. I. Title.
    BF431.3.C35 1998
    153.9'3--dc22
                            2007048413

Typeset by Saxon Graphics Ltd, Derby
Printed and bound in India by Replika Press Pvt Ltd

Contents

Introduction   1

1   IQ Test One   5
2   IQ Test Two   15
3   IQ Test Three   27
4   IQ Test Four   39
5   IQ Test Five   49
6   IQ Test Six   61
7   IQ Test Seven   73
8   IQ Test Eight   85
9   IQ Test Nine   97
10 IQ Test Ten   109
11 IQ Test Eleven   121
12 IQ Test Twelve   133

Answers, Explanations and Assessment   145

Introduction

In several of my earlier Kogan Page titles I have provided readers with the opportunity to obtain a greater understanding of IQ testing by means of practice tests in which readers have been able to familiarize themselves with the type of questions they are likely to encounter when taking such tests.

In this book I have retained some of the question types that have appeared in my previous books but have also introduced several new types of questions designed to measure an advanced level of numerical, verbal and spatial ability, as well as questions involving the use of logical analysis, lateral thinking and problem-solving abilities. The object of this book, therefore, is to present readers with an even greater challenge in which the 12 separate tests have a higher than usual overall degree of difficulty.

Such tests are particularly useful to anyone who may need to undertake graduate and managerial selection in the future. They are also of value to any professional who contemplates seeking other positions which may involve the use of psychometric testing as part of the selection process, or as a means of internal advancement in the organization in which they are employed.

The book will also appeal to people wishing to test themselves on more challenging questions by moving on from the standard-level IQ tests of previous books. These readers, who have already familiarized themselves with the type of IQ tests contained in my previous books, will now be ready to move on to a greater challenge.

As with athletes who push out the boundary of their abilities by the use of even more rigorous training schedules and refinement of techniques, an increase in brainpower can be achieved by taking on greater mental tasks and challenges. A further advantage to be gained from tackling the more advanced questions is that readers will automatically improve their performance on standard IQ test questions.

Because they have been newly compiled for this book, the tests that follow have not been standardized, so an actual IQ rating cannot be given. However, there is a guide to performance at the end of each test, and there is also a cumulative guide for your overall performance on all 12 tests. The performance assessment is particularly useful to users of this book as the feedback provided will give them the opportunity to identify their own strengths and weaknesses. This will enable readers to build on their strengths and work at improving their performance in areas of weakness.

Each test consists of 30 questions. The tests are all multidisciplinary, which provides the opportunity to practise on the range of questions you are likely to encounter in actual IQ tests.

A time limit of 120 minutes is allowed for each test. Answers and explanations, where necessary, are provided and you should award yourself one point for each completely correct answer.

The use of a calculator is not permitted in respect of the numerical questions, which are designed to test your aptitude when working with numbers as well as your powers of mental arithmetic.

Aspects of IQ testing

Of the different methods that purport to measure intelligence, the most famous is the IQ (Intelligence Quotient) test, which is a standardized test designed to measure human intelligence as distinct from attainments. Usually IQ tests consist of a graded series of tasks, each of which has been standardized with a large representative population of individuals in order to establish an average IQ of 100 for each test.

There are a number of different types of intelligence tests, for example Cattell, Stanford-Binet and Weschler, and each has its own different scale of intelligence.

It is generally accepted that a person's mental age remains constant in development to about the age of 13, after which it is shown to slow up, and beyond the age of 18 little or no improvement is found.

When the IQ of a child is measured the subject attempts an IQ test that has been standardized, with an average score recorded for each age group. Thus a 10-year-old child who scored the result that would be expected of a 12-year old would have an IQ of 120, or $(12 \div 10) \times 100$. Because after the age of 18 little or no improvement is found, adults have to be judged on an IQ test whose average score is 100 and the results graded above and below this norm according to known test scores.

Although it is generally accepted that it is not possible, in adulthood, to increase your actual IQ, it is possible, paradoxically, to improve your performance on IQ tests by practising on the various types of question, and learning to recognize the recurring themes. By constant practice on different IQ tests, and by getting your mind attuned to the different types of question you may encounter, it is possible to improve your IQ rating by several percentage points.

It should be pointed out that while IQ tests measure a variety of different types of ability such as verbal, mathematical, spatial and reasoning skills, it is now becoming increasingly recognized that there are many different types of intelligence and that a high measured IQ, although desirable, is not the only key to success in life. Other characteristics such as outstanding artistic, creative or practical prowess, especially if combined with personal characteristics such as ambition, good temperament and compassion, could result in an outstanding level of success despite a low measured IQ.

Nevertheless, during the past 25–30 years IQ testing, in tandem with personality profile testing, has been brought into widespread use by employers because of the need to ensure they place the right people in the right job at the outset. One of the main reasons for this is the high cost of errors in today's world of tight budgets and reduced profit margins. To recruit a new member of staff an employer has to advertise, consider each application, reduce the applicants to a shortlist, interview and then train the successful applicant. If the wrong hiring choice has been made, the whole expensive process has to be repeated.

Although it is IQ tests which we are specifically concerned with in this book, it should be pointed out that IQ tests are just one part of what is generally referred to as psychometric testing. Such test content may be addressed to almost any aspect of our intellectual or emotional make-up, including personality, attitude, intelligence or emotion.

Psychometric tests are basically tools used for measuring the mind: the word 'metric' means *measure* and the word 'psycho' means *mind*. There are two types of psychometric tests that are usually used in tandem by employers. These are aptitude tests which assess your abilities, and personality questionnaires which assess your character and personality.

Aptitude tests are also known as cognitive, ability or intelligence (IQ) tests. Such tests are designed to test your ability to comprehend quickly under strictly timed conditions. Cognition may be broadly defined as knowing, perceiving and thinking, and it is studied by psychologists because it reveals the extent of a person's ability to think.

IQ Test One

Circle the answer(s), or write in the answer box provided.

1.

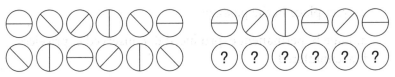

Which set of symbols should replace the question marks?

2. Select two words that are synonyms, plus an antonym of these two synonyms, from the list of words below.

   choke, force, thrive, toil, wither, burgeon, strive

3. 19, 20, 21, ?, ?, 26, 28, 32, 33, 40

   Which two numbers should replace the question marks?

   Answer [   ]

4. The institution houses collections of objects of artistic, historic and scientific interest, and displayed for the edification and enjoyment of the public.

   One word has been removed from the passage above. Select that word from the choice below and reinstate it into its correct place in the passage.

   a. huge b. permanent c. produced d. conserved e. priceless f. accumulated

5. Which is the odd one out?

   congregation, dispersion, compilation, convocation, aggregation

6. Ω # – Ω Ω # # – ? Ω # – Ω Ω # # – = # Ω #

   – Ω Ω # # – ? Ω # – Ω Ω # # – = # Ω # – Ω

   Ω # # – ? Ω # – Ω Ω # # – Ω # – Ω Ω # # – ?

   Ω # – Ω Ω # # – = #

   Which two symbols are missing?

   a. Ω #   b. – Ω c. # #   d. = #   e. – =

7. Which number is the odd one out?

84129, 32418, 47632, 36119, 67626, 72927

8. Identify two words (one from each set of brackets) that form a connection (analogy), thereby relating to the words in capitals in the same way.

CAT (lash, parade, feline, whiskers)

SLEEP (somnambulate, night, bed, Morpheus)

9. Which word in brackets is closest in meaning to the word in capitals?

FLIPPANT (obverse, irreverent, feeble, candid, facile)

10.   12593   is to   35291

     and   29684   is to   46982

     therefore 72936   is to   ?

                                              Answer [   ]

11. $\dfrac{99}{?} = 24.75 \times 2^4$

Complete the equation by correctly identifying the missing part of the calculation from the list of options below.

a. 0.75   b. 1.95 – 0.75   c. 0.5^2 d. 0.825   e. 0.25

12.

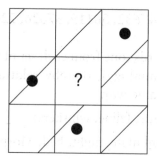

Draw the contents of the middle tile in accordance with the rules of logic already established.

13. Insert numbers into the remaining blank squares so that the sums in each line and column are correct. All numbers to be inserted are less than 10.

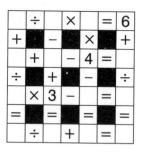

14. Identify a pair of anagrams from the list of words below.

intercom, carolean, fornical, landrace, alderman, maladies, parlance, calendar, marlined, miracles, minerals, confined, barnacle

15. A Z B Y D W G T ? ?

Which two letters come next?   Answer [   ]

16.

14	27	56	18	76	32		68	64	71	19	25	49
5	9	11	9	13	5		?	?	?	?	?	?

The top set of six numbers has a relationship to the set of six numbers below. The two sets of six boxes on the left have the same relationship as the two sets of six boxes on the right. Which set of numbers should therefore replace the question marks?

A

14	4	8	8	5	7

B

16	9	4	10	3	13

C

12	9	4	18	6	19

D

12	10	9	8	5	7

E

14	10	8	10	7	13

17. How many cases do you need if you have to pack 112 pairs of shoes into cases that each hold 28 shoes?

Answer [   ]

18. Which is the odd one out?

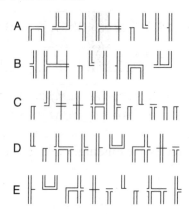

19. In the two numerical sequences below, one number that appears in the top sequence should appear in the bottom sequence and vice versa. Which two numbers should be changed round?

2, 2.5, 4.5, 6.75

1, 3, 6.25, 15.625

20.

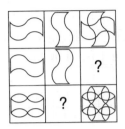

Which two squares are missing?

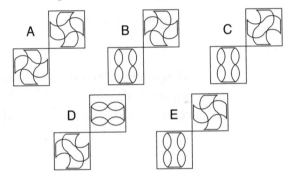

21. Identify two words (one from each set of brackets) that form a connection (analogy), thereby relating to the words in capitals in the same way.

FRONT (inverse, ulterior, anterior, contraverse, obverse)

FACE (exterior, converse, countenance, obverse)

22. Change the position of four words only in the sentence below in order for it to make complete sense.

If you are printing on glossy paper or transparencies, place a support stack, or a sheet of plain media, beneath the sheet, or load only one sheet at a time.

23. $? + (350 \times 0.84) = (620 \times 0.55) - \dfrac{\sqrt{1764}}{2}$

Complete the equation by correctly identifying the missing part of the calculation from the list of options below.

a. 13.5×2 b. $\dfrac{234}{9} + 1$ c. $3^3 + 1$ d. $\dfrac{120 \times 65\%}{3}$ e. $\dfrac{61}{17} \times 2^2$

24. Which two words are most opposite in meaning?

acquired, derivative, archetypal, elaborate, enigmatic, spasmodic

25. Select two words that are synonyms, plus an antonym of these two synonyms, from the list of words below.

excuse, regulate, bestow, condone, concede, condemn, incarcerate

26. Which is the odd one out?

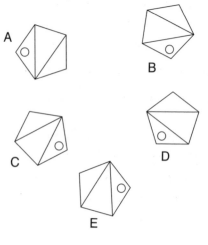

27. If 4 apples and 6 bananas cost £1.56 and 9 apples and 7 bananas cost £2.60, what is the cost of one apple and one banana?

Answer [   ]

28. An electrical circuit wiring a set of four lights depends on a system of switches A, B, C and D. Each switch when working has the following effect on the lights:

Switch A turns lights 1 and 2 on/off or off/on

Switch B turns lights 2 and 4 on/off or off/on

Switch C turns lights 1 and 3 on/off or off/on

Switch D turns lights 3 and 4 on/off or off/on

In the following, switches C B D A are thrown in turn, with the result that Figure 1 is transformed into Figure 2. One of the switches is therefore not working and has had no effect on the numbered lights.

Identify which one of the switches is not working.

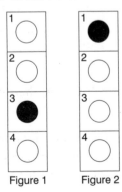

Figure 1   Figure 2

29.

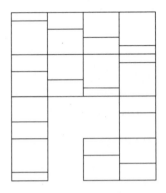

Which is the missing section?

A

B

C

D

30. _____ _____ is used for a _____ variety of _____,
including the _____ of _____ data for oil and _____
_____, the _____ of new _____ designs, the processing
of _____ _____, and the _____ of data from _____
_____.

Insert the 15 words below into their correct position in the
above passage.

analysis, analysis, applications, data, experiments,
exploration, imagery, mineral, processing, processing,
product, satellite, seismic, scientific, wide

IQ Test Two

Circle the answer(s), or write in the answer box provided.

1.

50	51	49	52	48
46	47	45	48	44
49	50		51	
47		46		45
48		47	50	46

Which is the missing section?

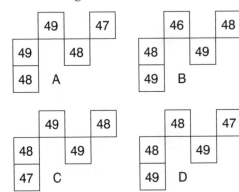

2. An electrical circuit wiring a set of four lights depends on a system of switches A, B, C and D. Each switch when working has the following effect on the lights:

Switch A turns lights 1 and 2 on/off or off/on

Switch B turns lights 2 and 4 on/off or off/on

Switch C turns lights 1 and 3 on/off or off/on

Switch D turns lights 3 and 4 on/off or off/on

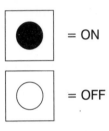

In the following, switches B C A D are thrown in turn, with the result that Figure 1 is transformed into Figure 2. One of the switches is therefore not working and has had no effect on the numbered lights.

Identify which one of the switches is not working.

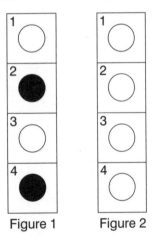

Figure 1   Figure 2

3. Starting from North, list the following compass points in the correct order working anti-clockwise.

    ENE WSW SE SSW WNW NNE SSE ESE

---

4. Insert the numbers listed into the circles so that – for any particular circle – the sum of the numbers in the circles connected to it equals the value corresponding to that circled number in the list. For example:

$1 = 14 (4 + 7 + 3)$

$3 = 1$

$4 = 8 (1 + 7)$

$7 = 5 (1 + 4)$

$1 = 12$

$2 = 4$

$3 = 12$

$4 = 8$

$5 = 8$

$6 = 3$

5. Which word in brackets is most opposite in meaning to the word in capitals?

    REPLETE (open, barren, energetic, inviting, satiated)

6. Select two words that are synonyms, plus an antonym of these two synonyms, from the list of words below.

    spearhead, escort, vanguard, patrol, weapon, stern, space

7.

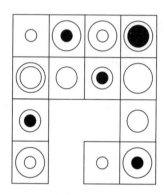

Which is the missing section?

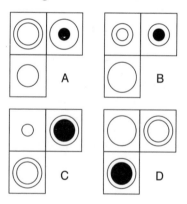

8. Use each letter of the phrase CLEAR TRIUMPH PATTERN once only to produce the names of three musical instruments.

9. In the two numerical sequences below, one number that appears in the top sequence should appear in the bottom sequence and vice versa. Which two numbers should be changed round?

    100, 89, 76, 63, 44, 25

    105, 93, 79, 61, 45, 25

10. Which word below is out of sequence?

    manage, aplomb, fedora, manual, jumble, junior, author

11.

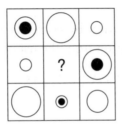

    Draw the contents of the middle tile in accordance with the rules of logic already established.

12. What number is, logically, missing from the sequence below?

    348269, 284315, *****, 8438, 4811, 842, 86

    Answer [   ]

13. Change the position of four words only in the sentence below in order for it to make complete sense.

    Soil rises from the material of the maple tree in the form of crude sap, a solution of sap that is absorbed from root.

14. 4, 45, 11.3, 41.3, ?, ?, 25.9, 33.9

Which two numbers should replace the question marks?

Answer [   ]

15. Identify two words (one from each set of brackets) that form a connection (analogy), thereby relating to the words in capitals in the same way.

LUMBER (arm, timber, back, neck)

TIBIAL (knee, leg, brain, drum)

16. $\frac{56 \times 3}{8} = \sqrt{49} \times$?

Complete the equation by correctly identifying the missing part of the calculation from the list of options below.

a. $\frac{276}{92}$ b. $\sqrt{16}$ c. 3.25   d. $18 - \sqrt{196}$ e. $\frac{84 - 27}{3}$

17. Select two words that are synonyms, plus an antonym of these two synonyms, from the list of words below.

practicable, proficient, impossible, sensible, feasible, able, precise

18. Which does not belong in this sequence?

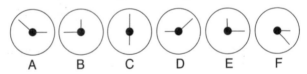

A   B   C   D   E   F

19.

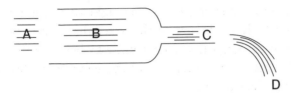

A large volume of water is gushing through a pipe which narrows at the outlet. At which point, A, B, C or D will the water flow fastest?

Answer

20.

Which three symbols are missing?

A

B

C

D

E

21. A   B   C   D   E   F   G   H

What letter comes two to the right of the letter which is immediately to the left of the letter that comes three to the right of the letter that comes midway between the letter two to the left of the letter C and the letter immediately to the right of the letter F?

Answer _____

22. $\dfrac{46}{2.5} \times 5 = \dfrac{?}{0.125}$

Complete the equation by correctly identifying the missing part of the calculation from the list of options below.

a. 5.75×2 b. 11.75 c. $2.25^2 \times 2$ d. 2.75×4
e. $15.75 - 3$

23. Which two words are closest in meaning?

Secure, masticate, allow, gnaw, twist, mete

24.

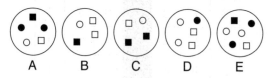

Which circle below should replace the question mark?

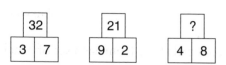

A   B   C   D   E

25.

32
3	7

21
9	2

?
4	8

What number should replace the question mark?

Answer [   ]

26. What is: $6\frac{1}{4} \div 3\frac{3}{8}$?

Answer [   ]

27. It is a largely agricultural country of varied scenery from moorland, loughs and islands to the beautiful coastline around West Bay.

    One word has been removed from the passage above. Select that word from the choice below and reinstate it into its correct place in the passage.

    a. landlocked b. eastern c. diverse d. cold e. oceanic f. bleak

28. Each set of nine numbers relates to the other in a certain way. Work out the logic behind the numbers in the left-hand box in order to determine which number is missing from the right-hand box.

3	7	2		6	7	1
1	5	4		3	?	4
2	9	4		1	2	1

Answer [   ]

29. Identify two words (one from each set of brackets) that form a connection (analogy), thereby relating to the words in capitals in the same way.

    PACHYDERM (tough, skin, ruminant, mammal)

    HIRSUTE (shaggy, course, wool, hair)

30.

Place four white circles correctly in the grid in accordance with the rules of logic already established.

IQ Test Three

Circle the answer(s), or write in the answer box provided.

1. Each set of nine numbers relates to the other in a certain way. Work out the logic behind the numbers in the left-hand box in order to determine which number is missing from the right-hand box.

3	5	9		4	2	7
9	6	6		3	8	2
4	8	2		7	9	?

Answer [   ]

2. Change the position of three words only in the sentence below in order for it to make complete sense.

    Because housing is necessary for everyone, the problem of providing adequate individuals has long been a concern, not only of shelter but also of governments.

3.   SUNDAY

     MONDAY

     TUESDAY

     WEDNESDAY

     THURSDAY

     FRIDAY

     SATURDAY

What day comes three days after the day which comes two days after the day which comes immediately after the day which comes two days after Monday?

Answer

4.   Select two words that are synonyms, plus an antonym of these two synonyms, from the list of words below.

prosaic, equitable, fascinating, predictive, unequal, benign, mundane

5.   What is the value of –26 – –37?

Answer

6.

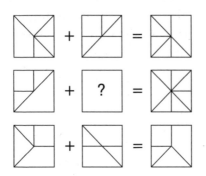

Which is the missing square?

A   B   C   D   E

7. Identify two words (one from each set of brackets) that form a connection (analogy), thereby relating to the words in capitals in the same way.

PAR (standard, able, golf, rank)

LEG (foot, bow, self, end)

8. Insert the numbers listed into the circles so that – for any particular circle – the sum of the numbers in the circles connected to it equals the value corresponding to that circled number in the list. For example:

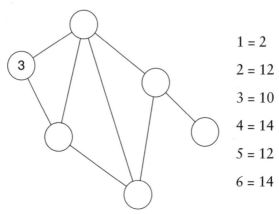

$1 = 14 (4 + 7 + 3)$

$3 = 1$

$4 = 8 (1 + 7)$

$7 = 5 (1 + 4)$

$1 = 2$

$2 = 12$

$3 = 10$

$4 = 14$

$5 = 12$

$6 = 14$

9. $$\frac{69 \times 32}{2^3} = ? \times \frac{48}{3}$$

Complete the equation by correctly identifying the missing part of the calculation from the list of options below.

a. $\dfrac{35}{2}$ b. 16.75 c. 17.25 d. $4^2 + 1.5$ e. 12×1.5

10. An electrical circuit wiring a set of four lights depends on a system of switches A, B, C and D. Each switch when working has the following effect on the lights:

Switch A turns lights 1 and 2 on/off or off/on

Switch B turns lights 2 and 4 on/off or off/on

Switch C turns lights 1 and 3 on/off or off/on

Switch D turns lights 3 and 4 on/off or off/on

● = ON

○ = OFF

In the following, switches C A B D are thrown in turn, with the result that Figure 1 is transformed into Figure 2. One of the switches is therefore not working and has had no effect on the numbered lights.

Identify which one of the switches is not working.

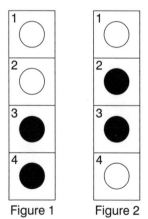

Figure 1   Figure 2

11.   23694   is to   64239

    and   821543   is to   842135

    therefore   72915638   is to   ?

                                              Answer [   ]

12. Identify two words (one from each set of brackets) that form
    a connection (analogy), thereby relating to the words in
    capitals in the same way.

    PAINT (brush, colour, dry, pigment)

    CONCRETE (solid, set, sand, road)

13.

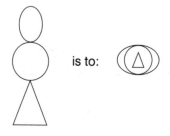

is to:

as:

is to:

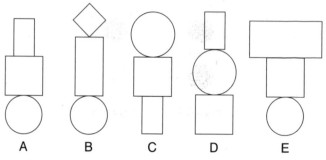

14. In the two numerical sequences below, one number that appears in the top sequence should appear in the bottom sequence and vice versa. Which two numbers should be changed round?

16, 39, 63, 90, 120

18, 36, 60, 88, 120

15. Although he did not enter the bank, he drove the getaway car, which makes him an accessory before the fact.

One word has been removed from the passage above. Select that word from the choice below and reinstate it into its correct place in the passage.

a. possibly b. down c. prime d. unfortunately e. legally
f. sometimes

16.

Which symbol is missing?

A ♠
B ♦
C ♣
D ♥

17. Which two words are closest in meaning?

joint, obese, corporal, genial, physical, harsh

18. If Milly gives Tilly £60 the money they have is in the ratio 2:1; however, if Tilly gives Milly £10 the ratio is 1:3. How much money have Milly and Tilly before they exchange any money?

Answer

19.

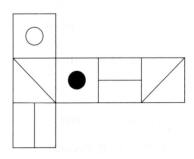

When the above is folded to form a cube, just **two** of the following can be produced. Which two?

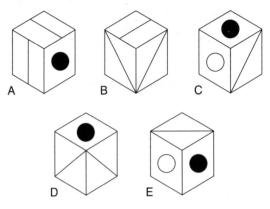

20. 10, 10, 9, 7, 7, ?, 4, 4, 3, 1

What number should replace the question mark?

Answer

21. Select two words that are synonyms, plus an antonym of these two synonyms, from the list of words below.

    sanction, define, proscribe, impel, boycott, check, articulate

22. $\dfrac{13 \times 82}{4} = 0.125 \times$?

    Complete the equation by correctly identifying the missing part of the calculation from the list of options below.

    a. 2132   b. 59×36 c. 8696   d. $\dfrac{2312}{2^2}$ e. 58×36

23. Which logically is the odd one out?

    dosage, before, volume, simple, curate

24.

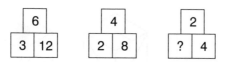

What number should replace the question mark?

                                Answer [   ]

25.

Which one of the figures below can be formed by rotating the figure above?

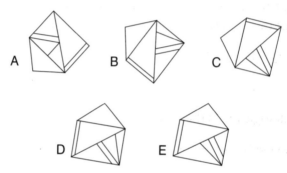

26. Gordon is twice as old as Tony was when Gordon was as old as Tony is now.

The combined age of Gordon and Tony is 112 years. How old are Gordon and Tony now?

Answer

27. Using every letter of the phrase GIBBON CABLES ACE COBRA once each only spell out the names of three vegetables.

_____

28. What word in brackets is most opposite in meaning to the word in capitals?

REVOKE (modify, conserve, exalt, implement, countermand)

29. The time is 14 minutes to the hour on a clock in which the numbers on the face are shown in Roman numerals. Arrange the numerals below in the order in which they appear from the minute hand reading anti-clockwise.

   III   XI   VII   IX   IV

30. Which three of the four pieces below can be fitted together to form a perfect square?

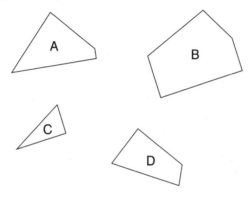

4

IQ Test Four

Circle the answer(s), or write in the answer box provided.

1. I WINE ON VIP OPTION is an anagram of which two words that are similar in meaning (7, 9 letters long)?

_____

2. 329 : 15

   746 : 34

   Which numbers below have the same relationship to each other as the two sets of numbers above?

   a. 287 : 22 b. 698 : 62 c. 942 : 68 d. 382 : 12 e. 749 : 35

3.

♪♦♫♥♪♣♫♠♪☺♪♦♫♥♪♣♫♠♪☺♪♦♫♥♪♣♫

♠♪☺♪♦♫♥♪♣♫♠♪☺♪♪♫♥♪♣♫♠♪☺♪♦♫♥♪

♣♫♠♪☺♦♫♥♪♣♫♠♪☺♪♦♫♥♪♣♫♠♪☺♪♦♫♥

♪♣♫♠♪☺

Which symbol is missing?

A ☺
B ♫
C ♣
D ♪
C ♥

4. Place two letters in each set of brackets so that they form a word when tacked onto the letters on the left and form another word when placed in front of the letters on the right. The letters placed in the brackets must produce an eight-letter word when read downwards in pairs.

HE	(**)	LY
HO	(**)	AR
AU	(**)	NK
CO	(**)	CH

5.

$$? + 58 = \frac{5^4 \times 60\%}{\sqrt{81} - \sqrt{16}}$$

Complete the equation by correctly identifying the missing part of the calculation from the list of options below.

a. $51 \times \dfrac{3}{9}$ b. $3^3 - 2^3$ c. $70\% \times 27$ d. 2.5×7 e. 16.5

6.

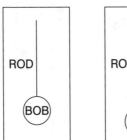 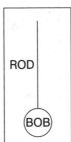

Which of the following factors is most likely to determine that the pendulums on the two clocks will swing back and forth at exactly the same rate?

a. the size of the pendulum arc

b. the length of the rod or string

c. the weight of the bob

d. the synchronicity of the timekeeping of the two clocks

7.   Which is the larger fraction?

$$\frac{3}{7} \qquad \frac{13}{28} \qquad \frac{5}{14}$$

8. Identify two words (one from each set of brackets) that form a connection (analogy), thereby relating to the words in capitals in the same way.

    HEADLONG (giddy, wild, gung-ho, frantic)

    IMPRUDENT (heedless, impetuous, madcap, confused)

9.

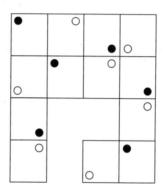

Which is the missing section?

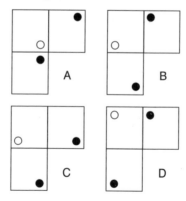

10. Select two words that are synonyms, plus an antonym of these two synonyms, from the list of words below.

decant, harangue, crumble, debilitate, weaken, dishonour, invigorate

11. $3^2 + 27^2 = ?$

Complete the equation by correctly identifying the missing part of the calculation from the list of options below.

a. $1242 - 505$ b. $1478 \div 2$ c. $1232 \times 60\%$ d. $\dfrac{12546}{17}$ e. $\dfrac{84^2}{9}$

12. Change the position of three words only in the sentence below in order for it to make complete sense.

Imaginary in the Middle Ages, a Bestiary is a type of book that purports to describe all the animals in creation, real or human, and the popular traits they exemplify.

13. A bag of potatoes weighs 50 lbs divided by half of its weight. How much does the bag of potatoes weigh?

Answer [   ]

14. Which word in brackets is closest in meaning to the word in capitals?

HERMETIC (sealed, reclusive, audacious, sceptic, close)

15.

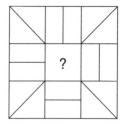

Draw the contents of the middle tile in accordance with the rules of logic already established.

16. In the two numerical sequences below, one number that appears in the top sequence should appear in the bottom sequence and vice versa. Which two numbers should be changed round?

2, 5, 11, 15, 47

3, 7, 23, 31, 63

17. A   B   C   D   E   F   G   H

What letter comes three to the right of the letter that comes immediately to the left of the letter that comes three to the right of the letter immediately to the left of the letter B?

Answer [   ]

18. How many minutes is it before 12 noon if 1 hour 39 minutes ago it was twice as many minutes past 8 am?

Answer [   ]

19. Which word in brackets is most opposite in meaning to the word in capitals?

INDIGENT (rich, peaceful, eager, decorous, powerful)

20. Which does not belong in this sequence?

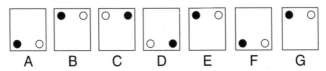

21. Select two words that are synonyms, plus an antonym of these two synonyms, from the list of words below.

innovative, obstinate, strained, tractable, willing, accessible, brief

22. What number should replace the question mark?

4	2	2	2
3	1	1	4
3	2	1	5
2	3	4	?

Answer [   ]

23. Which word does not logically belong in the list below?

glance, anchor, charge, casino, arcade

24. Complete the pattern in accordance with the rules of logic already established.

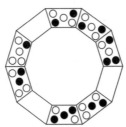

25.

12	3	7	8	10	18		4	11	2	5	6	13
6	6	14	4	5	9		?	?	?	?	?	?

The top set of six numbers has a relationship to the set of six numbers below. The two sets of six boxes on the left have the same relationship as the two sets of six boxes on the right. Which set of numbers should therefore replace the question marks?

A | 8 | 6 | 4 | 10 | 3 | 22 |

B | 2 | 22 | 1 | 10 | 3 | 26 |

C | 8 | 22 | 4 | 8 | 12 | 5 |

D | 2 | 5 | 6 | 13 | 11 | 4 |

E | 6 | 6 | 1 | 10 | 12 | 26 |

26. The shop is a delight to travellers as it is prepared to outfit anyone for anything, from a walk in the country to an African safari or an Arctic expedition.

One word has been removed from the passage above. Select that word from the choice below and reinstate it into its correct place in the passage.

a. accomplished b. strenuous c. open d. prospective e. often f. substantially

27. An electrical circuit wiring a set of four lights depends on a system of switches A, B, C and D. Each switch when working has the following effect on the lights:

Switch A turns lights 1 and 2 on/off or off/on

Switch B turns lights 2 and 4 on/off or off/on

Switch C turns lights 1 and 3 on/off or off/on

Switch D turns lights 3 and 4 on/off or off/on

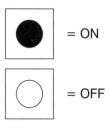

= ON

= OFF

In the following, switches D A B C are thrown in turn, with the result that Figure 1 is transformed into Figure 2. One of the switches is therefore not working and has had no effect on the numbered lights.

Identify which one of the switches is not working.

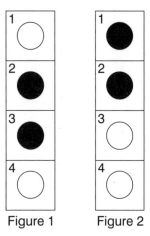

Figure 1   Figure 2

28. 24, 30, ? , 60, 84, 114

What number should replace the question mark?

Answer

29. Identify two words (one from each set of brackets) that form a connection (analogy), thereby relating to the words in capitals in the same way.

AMASS (gather, salvage, sustain, keep)

CONSERVE (retrieve, stockpile, protect, reclaim)

30.

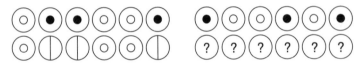

Which set of symbols should replace the question marks?

IQ Test Five

Circle the answer(s), or write in the answer box provided.

1. Which is the odd one out?

   A   ¥ « £ ¢ µ ¶ ▶ *

   B   Π µ ¶ £ ▶ Ω ✿ ♪

   C   Ω & Π ✿ ♪ fl µ ¶

   D   * ▶ ¶ µ ¢ £ « ¥

   E   ¶ µ fl ♪ ✿ Π & Ω

2.

   What number should replace the question mark?

   Answer [   ]

3.   An electrical circuit wiring a set of four lights depends on a system of switches A, B, C and D. Each switch when working has the following effect on the lights:

Switch A turns lights 1 and 2 on/off or off/on

Switch B turns lights 2 and 4 on/off or off/on

Switch C turns lights 1 and 3 on/off or off/on

Switch D turns lights 3 and 4 on/off or off/on

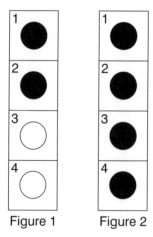

● = ON

○ = OFF

In the following, switches C A D B are thrown in turn, with the result that Figure 1 is transformed into Figure 2. One of the switches is therefore not working and has had no effect on the numbered lights.

Identify which one of the switches is not working.

Figure 1   Figure 2

4. 1, 2, 0, 3, ?, 4, ?

    What two numbers should replace the question marks?

    Answer [   ]

5. Identify two words (one from each set of brackets) that form a connection (analogy), thereby relating to the words in capitals in the same way.

    QUIRKY (bizarre, irrational, whimsical, erratic)

    UNCANNY (singular, eerie, esoteric, amazing)

6. Select two words that are synonyms, plus an antonym of these two synonyms, from the list of words below.

    torment, contain, consider, console, assuage, scheme, fraternize

7. In the two numerical sequences below, one number that appears in the top sequence should appear in the bottom sequence and vice versa. Which two numbers should be changed round?

    3, 6, 9.5, 14.5, 18, 23

    5, 10, 13.5, 18.5, 22

8. Which word in brackets is closest in meaning to the word in capitals?

    CHAGRIN (reprehension, revolution, irritation, bedlam, assault)

9.

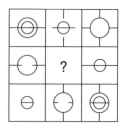

Draw the contents of the middle tile in accordance with the rules of logic already established.

10.
1	2	4	2
3	6	12	18
1	10	28	58
2	13	51	?

What number should replace the question mark?

Answer [   ]

11. Only one group of six letters below can be rearranged to spell out a six-letter word in the English language. Identify the word.

NITLAF

IFCLEA

AHGOLI

OLKECM

FITRAB

RNUMLA

12.
$$639 + ? = 2 \times \frac{582 + 381}{3}$$

Complete the equation by correctly identifying the missing part of the calculation from the list of options below.

a. 0.25×11 b. $1.5^3 - 0.125$ c. $\frac{\sqrt{81}}{3}$ d. $\sqrt{100} - \frac{9}{3}$ e. $6^2 \div 9$

13. Which two words are most opposite in meaning?

virtuous, impecunious, calm, nefarious, nonchalant, fastidious

14.

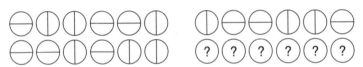

Which set of diagrams below should replace the question marks?

15. Change the position of five words only in the sentence below in order for it to make complete sense.

    If customers like the goods, the product enables them to dislike what to look for in the trademark; if they know the future they will avoid goods with that trademark.

16. Insert numbers into the remaining blank squares so that the sums in each line and column are correct. All numbers to be inserted are less than 10.

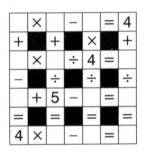

17. Which is the odd one out?

    puissant, anodyne, cogent, definitive, trenchant

18.

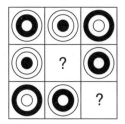

Which two squares are missing?

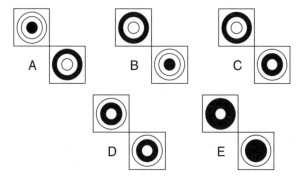

19. The average of three numbers is 29. The average of two of these numbers is 38. What is the third number?

Answer [   ]

20. A relatively thin envelope, the atmosphere consists of layers of gases that support life and provide protection from radiation.

One word has been removed from the passage above. Select that word from the choice below and reinstate it into its correct place in the passage.

a. hot b. deep c. harmful d. diffused e. moderate f. toxic

21.

&&●&&&○&&&&●&&&○&&●&&&○&&&&

●&&&○&&●&&&○&&&&●&&&○

&&&○&&&&●&&&○

Which three symbols are missing?

A   &●&

B   ●&&

C   &&&

D   &&●

E   &○&

22. Public _____ _____ sell their _____ to the
_____ _____, whereas _____ companies
_____ _____ shares to, or _____ _____
_____ , the general public.

Insert the 11 words below into their correct position in the above passage.

can, cannot, companies, from, general, money, private, public, raise, sell, shares

23.

4	8	2	3	9	7		5	9	1	4	3	6
2	9	4	7	3	8		?	?	?	?	?	?

The top set of six numbers has a relationship to the set of six numbers below. The two sets of six boxes on the left have the same relationship as the two sets of six boxes on the right. Which set of numbers should therefore replace the question marks?

A | 4 | 5 | 3 | 1 | 9 | 5 |

B | 1 | 3 | 5 | 6 | 4 | 9 |

C | 9 | 5 | 1 | 6 | 3 | 4 |

D | 8 | 2 | 7 | 9 | 3 | 6 |

E | 2 | 4 | 8 | 1 | 3 | 5 |

24. Identify two words (one from each set of brackets) that form a connection (analogy), thereby relating to the words in capitals in the same way.

ANSER (duck, owl, goose, eagle)

CORVUS (falcon, pelican, crane, crow)

25.

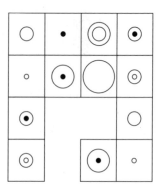

Which is the missing section?

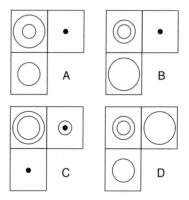

26. 535 : 7580 : 852

483 : 9642 : 716

723 :   ?   : 633

What number should logically replace the question mark?

Answer ☐

27. HILT is to LMPY

as DENS is to ????   Answer [   ]

28. $\dfrac{74}{9.25} \times 4.5 = \dfrac{? \times 6}{2}$

Complete the equation by correctly identifying the missing part of the calculation from the list of options below.

a. $\sqrt{144} + 1.5^2$ b. $\sqrt{144}$ c. $\sqrt{169}$ d. 11.5 e. $2^3 \times 2.5$

29. Select two words that are synonyms, plus an antonym of these two synonyms, from the list of words below.

brackish, crisp, bold, sinewy, unpolluted, bright, undrinkable

30.

 ?

What comes next in the above sequence?

A   B   C   D   E

6

IQ Test Six

Circle the answer(s), or write in the answer box provided.

1. A B C D E F G H

   What letter is two to the right of the letter which is four to the
   left of the letter which is immediately to the right of the letter
   four to the right of the letter C?

   Answer

2. In a right-angled triangle, what is the length of the shortest
   side if the length of the hypotenuse is 65 cm and the length of
   the second-longest side is 63 cm?

   Answer

3.

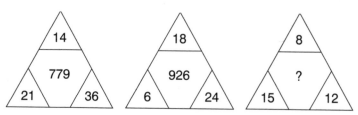

   What number should replace the question mark?

   Answer

4.

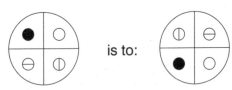

as:

is to:

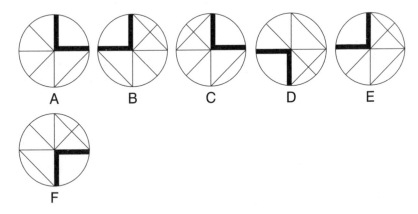

5. Carrie has 0.125 more than Larry and Larry has ¾ more than Harry. Between them Harry, Larry and Carrie have 151. How many has each?

Answer [   ]

6.   Change the position of six words only in the sentence below in order for it to make complete sense.

Like the patterns which occur in seasons, such as the heart of the planets, the succession of nature, and the beating of the motion, musical rhythm is usually organized in regularly recurring rhythms.

7.   7382961   is to   2016

     and   3864987   is to   2124

     therefore   7958279   is to   ?

                                              Answer [   ]

8.   Each set of nine numbers relates to the other in a certain way. Work out the logic behind the numbers in the left-hand box in order to determine which number is missing from the right-hand box.

4	9	8		6	8	7
8	7	7		9	7	3
3	7	9		2	8	?

                                              Answer [   ]

9.   Which is the odd one out?

     catwalk, gallery, apron, wings, proscenium

10. Which is the odd one out?

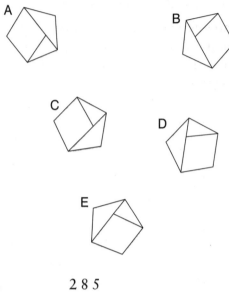

11.   6 4 2   2 8 5

      9 8 7   is to   8 7 3

      3 9 4   3 6 1

as 4 9 6   is to   7 2 3

      3 7 2   ? ? ?

      8 5 3   ? ? ?

Answer [   ]

12. Select two words that are synonyms, plus an antonym of these two synonyms, from the list of words below.

natural, gracious, sudden, charitable, impolite, delicate, idle

13. What is the factorial of 5?

a. 1   b. 120   c. 60   d. 25   e. 15

14. Identify two words (one from each set of brackets) that form a connection (analogy), thereby relating to the words in capitals in the same way.

    ENTRANCE (door, antechamber, admittance, access)

    EXIT (egress, escape, vanish, stairway)

15. Which is the odd one out?

    A ◀#●&*▼#◀◀Ω●○○▶◀◀
       ◀#●&▼
       ▼#Ω●○○▶◀

    B ◀#●&*▼▼#◀◀Ω●○***○▶◀◀
       ◀#●&▼
       ▼#Ω●○○▶◀

    C ◀#●&*▼▼#◀◀Ω●○***○▶◀◀
       ◀#●&▼
       ▼#Ω●○○▶◀

    D ◀#●&*▼▼#◀◀Ω●○○▶◀◀
       ◀#●&▼
       ▼#Ω●○○▶◀

    E ◀#●&*▼#◀◀Ω●○○▶◀◀
       ◀#●&▼
       ▼#Ω●○○▶◀

16. $\dfrac{\sqrt{81}\,(\times 7)}{\sqrt{(12.5\% \times 72)}} = \dfrac{1}{4}$?

    Complete the equation by correctly identifying the missing part of the calculation from the list of options below.

    a. $9^2 + 5$ b. $\dfrac{5}{9} \times 144$ c. $(197 - 112)$ d. $\dfrac{77}{11} \times 14$ e. $(177 - 93)$

17. In the two numerical sequences below, one number that appears in the top sequence should appear in the bottom sequence and vice versa. Which two numbers should be changed round?

    10, 20, 60, 180, 360, 720

    10, 30, 60, 120, 360, 1080

18. Which two words are closest in meaning?

    farcical, improper, wise, prolific, wild, risible

19. Which of the following is not an anagram of a type of fruit?

    rip coat

    ova coda

    burly beer

    real madam

    pipe panel

    alert women

    part figure

20. Out of 384 guests at a conference, a quarter took their coffee with sugar only, $5/8$ took it with both milk and sugar, one out of every 16 guests took it with milk only and the rest took it black with neither milk nor sugar. How many guests took it black with neither milk nor sugar?

    Answer [   ]

21. The stiff, intricate branches form around the trunk and are covered with overlapping, scale-shaped leaves.

   One word has been removed from the passage above. Select that word from the choice below and reinstate it into its correct place in the passage.

   a. bark b. whorls c. green d. foliage e. tree f. stalks

22. 34, 48, ?, 79, 96

   What number should replace the question mark?

   Answer [   ]

23. Select two words that are synonyms, plus an antonym of these two synonyms, from the list of words below.

   mixed, suppressed, variable, firm, flexible, prodigious, microscopic

24.

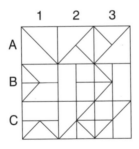

   Looking at lines across and down, if the first two tiles are combined to produce the third tile, with the exception that like lines or symbols are cancelled out, which of the above tiles is incorrect, and with which tile should it be replaced?

   A   B   C   D   E

25. FISCAL, SCRIBE, SELECT, INSIDE, MAYHEM, PURIFY, FLANGE

Logically, what word comes next?

GUILTY, RHYTHM, OXYGEN, PENCIL, THIRST

26. Insert the numbers listed into the circles so that – for any particular circle – the sum of the numbers in the circles connected to it equals the value corresponding to that circled number in the list. For example:

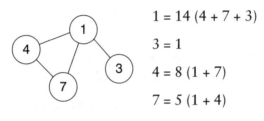

1 = 14 (4 + 7 + 3)

3 = 1

4 = 8 (1 + 7)

7 = 5 (1 + 4)

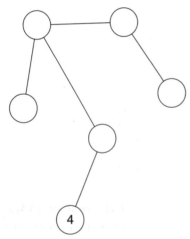

1 = 14

2 = 6

3 = 1

4 = 5

5 = 5

6 = 3

27. Identify two words (one from each set of brackets) that form a connection (analogy), thereby relating to the words in capitals in the same way.

THUNDEROUS SILENCE (simile, hyperbole, syllepsis, oxymoron)

REVERT BACK (tautology, metaphor, alliteration, metonymy)

28.

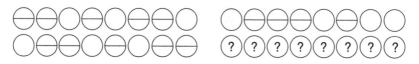

Which set of figures should replace the question marks?

29. An electrical circuit wiring a set of four lights depends on a system of switches A, B, C and D. Each switch when working has the following effect on the lights:

Switch A turns lights 1 and 2 on/off or off/on

Switch B turns lights 2 and 4 on/off or off/on

Switch C turns lights 1 and 3 on/off or off/on

Switch D turns lights 3 and 4 on/off or off/on

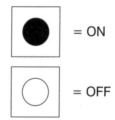

In the following, switches C B A D are thrown in turn, with the result that Figure 1 is transformed into Figure 2. One of the switches is therefore not working and has had no effect on the numbered lights.

Identify which one of the switches is not working.

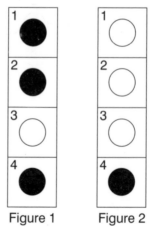

Figure 1   Figure 2

30. By making a single cut, divide the shape below into two identical (size and shape) pieces.

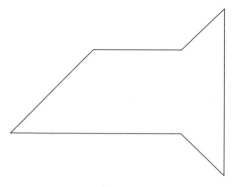

7

IQ Test Seven

Circle the answer(s), or write in the answer box provided.

1. What is:

$$\frac{17}{68} \text{ of } 12.5\% \text{ of } \frac{19}{57} \text{ of } \frac{30}{45} \text{ of } 144$$

Answer [ ]

2. Use every letter of the phrase PROPOUND RARE MAGIC once each only to spell out the names of three elements.

_____

3. At the end of the day one market stall had 16 apples and 48 oranges left. Another market stall had 36 apples and 24 oranges left. What is the difference between the percentages of apples left in the two market stalls?

Answer [ ]

4. Select two words that are synonyms, plus an antonym of these two synonyms, from the list of words below.

contrary, loyal, recalcitrant, compliant, imprudent, rash, withdrawn.

5. $$\frac{12.25 \times 8}{5\% \times 280} = \frac{25\% \times 532}{?}$$

Complete the equation by correctly identifying the missing part of the calculation from the list of options below.

a. $\dfrac{152}{9}$ b. 4.75×4 c. 3.5×5.5 d. $38 \div 2.5$ e. $17 + 2.5$

6.

Which of the figures below can be formed by rotating the figure above?

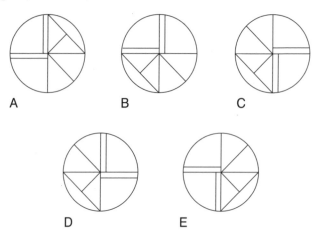

7. A   B   C   D   E   F   G   H

What letter is immediately to the left of the letter which is two to the left of the letter that comes midway between the letter two to the right of the letter F and the letter two to the left of the letter D?

Answer [   ]

8. Her novels reflect her background, highly allusive and in style, they draw their characters from academic and artistic works.

One word has been removed from the passage above. Select that word from the choice below and reinstate it into its correct place in the passage.

a. rich b. indirect c. written d. verbose e. literary f. strangely

9. What is the value of $\frac{3}{8} + \frac{5}{16}$ as a decimal?

Answer [   ]

10. Select two words that are synonyms, plus an antonym of these two synonyms, from the list of words below.

sphere, uniform, element, militia, miscellaneous, regalia, assorted

11. 100, 99.8, 99.2, ? , 92, 75.8

What number should replace the question mark?

Answer [   ]

12.

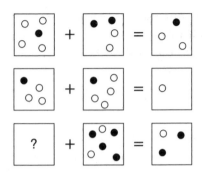

Which square below should replace the question mark?

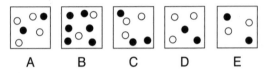

A   B   C   D   E

13. What is the longest word in the English language that can be produced from the ten letters below? No letter may be used more than once.

HTERCIKFAO

_____

14. Which is the odd one out?

INTEGRAL, ALTERING, TRIANGLE, REALIGNS, ALERTING

15. What is the value of 56 + −19?

Answer [   ]

16. Which two words are closest in meaning?

enticing, anodyne, seditious, mutinous, sealed, profane

17. Insert the numbers listed into the circles so that – for any particular circle – the sum of the numbers in the circles connected to it equals the value corresponding to that circled number in the list. For example:

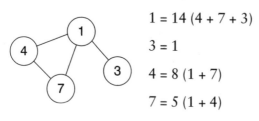

1 = 14 (4 + 7 + 3)

3 = 1

4 = 8 (1 + 7)

7 = 5 (1 + 4)

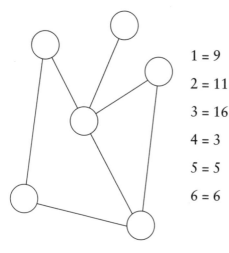

1 = 9

2 = 11

3 = 16

4 = 3

5 = 5

6 = 6

18.

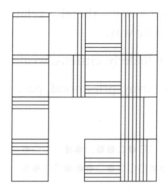

Which is the missing section?

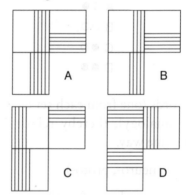

19. $\dfrac{5}{8} \div \dfrac{9}{16} = ?$

Complete the equation by correctly identifying the missing part of the calculation from the list of options below.

a. 0.9^2 b. $\dfrac{1000}{99}$ c. 1.01^2 d. $\dfrac{25}{22.5}$ e. 0.95^2

20. Identify two words (one from each set of brackets) that form a connection (analogy), thereby relating to the words in capitals in the same way.

PLUTOCRACY (elderly, citizens, wealthy, mob)

THEOCRACY (army, priesthood, party, ruler)

21.

○●●●○○●●○○○●○●●○●●○○○●○●●●○○●●○○

○●○●●●○○●●○○○●○●●●○○●●○○○●

Which two symbols are missing?

A ○●

B ○○

C ●○

D ●●

22. Identify two words (one from each set of brackets) that form a connection (analogy), thereby relating to the words in capitals in the same way.

NEW (bio-, neo-, neuro-, proto-)

OLD (ana-, haema-, palaeo-, ferro-)

23. In the two numerical sequences below, one number that appears in the top sequence should appear in the bottom sequence and vice versa. Which two numbers should be changed round?

24, 41, 62, 78, 98

14, 32, 48, 59, 74

24.

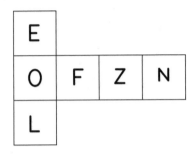

When the above is folded to form a cube, just two of the following can be produced. Which two?

25. Change the position of four words only in the sentence below in order for it to make complete sense.

Peacekeeping has always been conducted with the differences of the disputants, who at the very least agree to consent to settle their safety and not endanger the attempt of the peacekeeping forces.

26. 63 (97) 49

56 (73) 24

? (36) 54

What number should replace the question mark?

Answer [   ]

27. Which word in brackets is most opposite in meaning to the word in capitals?

PROTRUBERANT (brief, proud, concave, calm, smooth)

28. Each set of nine numbers relates to the other in a certain way. Work out the logic behind the numbers in the left-hand box in order to determine which number is missing from the right-hand box.

2	3	6		1	1	3
4	2	7		4	?	9
5	3	9		7	1	9

Answer [   ]

29. An electrical circuit wiring a set of four lights depends on a system of switches A, B, C and D. Each switch when working has the following effect on the lights:

Switch A turns lights 1 and 2 on/off or off/on

Switch B turns lights 2 and 4 on/off or off/on

Switch C turns lights 1 and 3 on/off or off/on

Switch D turns lights 3 and 4 on/off or off/on

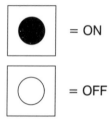

In the following, switches D C B A are thrown in turn, with the result that Figure 1 is transformed into Figure 2. One of the switches is therefore not working and has had no effect on the numbered lights.

Identify which one of the switches is not working.

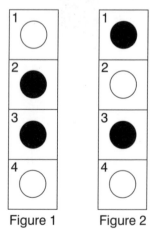

Figure 1   Figure 2

30. Which three pieces below can be fitted together to form a perfect square?

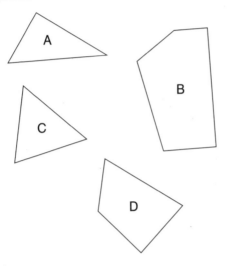

8

IQ Test Eight

Circle the answer(s), or write in the answer box provided.

1. The metal is in the form of a bar, either straight, or bent into the shape of a horseshoe.

    One word has been removed from the sentence above. Select that word from the choice below and reinstate it into its correct place in the passage.

    a. over b. across c. lucky d. shaped e. cylindrical f. generally

2.

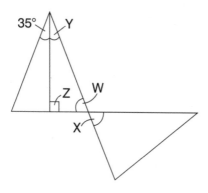

    What is the value of angle X?   Answer [   ]

3. Identify two words (one from each set of brackets) that form a connection (analogy), thereby relating to the words in capitals in the same way.

    TRIANGLE (height, radius, hypotenuse, angle)

    SQUARE (perimeter, diameter, area, tangent)

4.

6	4	2	5	4	1		7	2	4	3	5	6
9	8	5	9	7	5		?	?	?	?	?	?

The top set of six numbers has a relationship to the set of six numbers below. The two sets of six boxes on the left have the same relationship as the two sets of six boxes on the right. Which set of numbers should therefore replace the question marks?

A | 11 | 5 | 8 | 7 | 9 | 9 |

B | 9 | 7 | 6 | 8 | 7 | 11 |

C | 10 | 6 | 7 | 7 | 8 | 10 |

D | 10 | 6 | 7 | 8 | 9 | 11 |

E | 1 | 1 | 1 | 1 | 1 | 10 |

5.

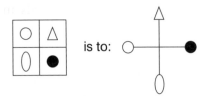

as:

is to:

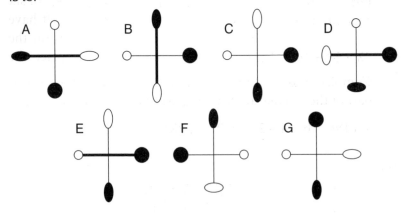

6. A _____ is a _____ _____ of two or more
    _____ who have _____ _____ to work together,
    each _____ skills, _____ and resources to the
    _____ in return for a _____ _____ of the
    _____ .

Insert the 12 words below into their correct position in the
above passage.

association, agreed, business, contributing, formally, labour,
partnership, people, pre-arranged, profits, share, venture

7. 3 2 8 4

    7 6 9 3

    9 5 6 4

    2 1 9 ?

What number should replace the question mark?

Answer [   ]

8. Select two words that are synonyms, plus an antonym of these two synonyms, from the list of words below.

punitive, wearisome, tiresome, energetic, exhilarating, arduous, tough

9. $58 \times 23 = 166.75 \times ?$

Complete the equation by correctly identifying the missing part of the calculation from the list of options below.

a. $\sqrt{196}$ b. $14 - 2^2$ c. 9   d. $\sqrt{81} - 2$ e. 2^3

10.

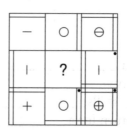

Draw the contents of the middle tile in accordance with the rules of logic already established.

11. An electrical circuit wiring a set of four lights depends on a system of switches A, B, C and D. Each switch when working has the following effect on the lights:

Switch A turns lights 1 and 2 on/off or off/on

Switch B turns lights 2 and 4 on/off or off/on

Switch C turns lights 1 and 3 on/off or off/on

Switch D turns lights 3 and 4 on/off or off/on

⬤ = ON

◯ = OFF

In the following, switches A D B C are thrown in turn, with the result that Figure 1 is transformed into Figure 2. One of the switches is therefore not working and has had no effect on the numbered lights.

Identify which one of the switches is not working.

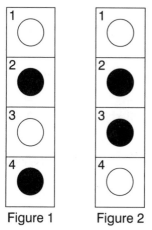

Figure 1   Figure 2

12. 7952 : 1211 : 23

Which set of numbers below has the same relationship to each other as the numbers above?

a. 3482 : 2408 : 16 b. 3496 : 1254 : 39 c. 8278 : 1510 : 25
d. 8217 : 9090 : 99 e. 9487 : 1612 : 37

13. Which is the odd one out?

A   %%%@+***$*++$$

B   *$*++$$%%%@+**

C   %@+***$*++$$%%

D $%%%@+***$+*+$

E   +$$%%@+***$*+

14. Which two words are most opposite in meaning?

pithy, serene, garrulous, amusing, inexorable, ostentatious

15. $\dfrac{1080}{?} = \sqrt{81} \times \sqrt{64}$

Complete the equation by correctly identifying the missing part of the calculation from the list of options below.

a. $5^2 - 8$ b. 13   c. $3^3 + 7$ d. 15   e. 14.75

16. Which word in brackets is closest in meaning to the word in capitals?

ESCHEW (conduct, avoid, amplify, escort, spout)

17.

$$*@\,?\,-\Omega\bullet\,\bullet\,*@+\,?\,-\Omega\bullet$$

$$\bullet\,*@+\,?\,-\Omega\bullet\,\bullet\,*@+\,?\,-$$

$$\Omega\bullet\,\bullet\,*@+\,?\,-\Omega\bullet\,\bullet$$

Which symbol is missing?

A ●

B Ω

C *

D +

E •

18. Change the position of four words only in the sentence below in order for it to make complete sense.

Instead of actively passive radio signals, some of the first communication equipment had no radio satellites aboard and were designed to operate in a transmitting mode.

19. Which is the odd one out?

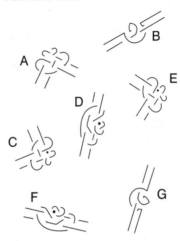

20. Identify the pair of anagrams from the list of words below.

    corniest, esoteric, serotine, ordinate, obtained, monsters, proteins, antipode, bisector, rationed, ptomaine, senorita, baritone

21. 105, 87, ?, 52, 35

    What number should replace the question mark?

    Answer [   ]

22. Which is the odd one out?

    abrogation, repeal, derogation, revocation, institute

23. $\dfrac{?}{18} = \dfrac{1087 - 422}{1.4 \times 5}$

Complete the equation by correctly identifying the missing part of the calculation from the list of options below.

a. $45\% \times 3800$ b. $(9 \times 5) \times 360$ c. $\dfrac{54^2}{36}$ d. 1080 e. $70^2 \div 2$

24.

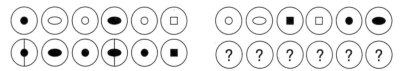

Which set of symbols should replace the question marks?

25. A, AB, ABD, ABDG, ABDGK, ??????

What group of letters comes next?

Answer [   ]

26. In a right-angled triangle, if the lengths of the two shortest sides are whole numbers exactly and the length of the hypotenuse is 40 cm, what are the lengths of the two shortest sides?

   Answer [   ]

27. Identify two words (one from each set of brackets) that form a connection (analogy), thereby relating to the words in capitals in the same way.

   PALMATE (finger, hand, tree, head)

   CORDATE (kidney, string, heart, horn)

28. Select two words that are synonyms, plus an antonym of these two synonyms, from the list of words below.

   engaging, unremarkable, bogus, arresting, apprehensive, undisguised, disdainful

29. In the two numerical sequences below, one number that appears in the top sequence should appear in the bottom sequence and vice versa. Which two numbers should be changed round?

   110, 90, 69, 45, 24, 0

   111, 90, 68, 47, 21, –4

30.

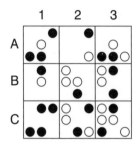

Looking at lines across and down, if the first two tiles are combined to produce the third tile, with the exception that like lines or symbols are cancelled out, which of the above tiles is incorrect, and with which tile should it be replaced?

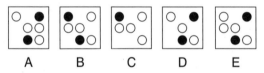

IQ Test Nine

Circle the answer(s), or write in the answer box provided.

1.
$$(68 + 42) \times ? = \frac{308}{5}$$

Complete the equation by correctly identifying the missing part of the calculation from the list of options below.

a. 48%   b. 56 %   c. 58%   d. 60%   e. 62%

2. You have two bags each containing six balls. The first bag contains balls numbered 1 to 6 and the second bag contains balls numbered 7 to 12. A ball is drawn out of bag one and another ball is drawn out of bag two. What are the chances that at least one of the balls drawn out is an odd-numbered ball?

Answer

3. Which word in brackets is most opposite in meaning to the word in capitals?

TACITURN (gauche, aggressive, indiscreet, unreserved, judicious)

4.

7	3	1	5	4	5		7	8	4	1	3	7
6	5	6	2	4	8		?	?	?	?	?	?

The top set of six numbers has a relationship to the set of six numbers below. The two sets of six boxes on the left have the same relationship as the two sets of six boxes on the right. Which set of numbers should therefore replace the question marks?

A	8	2	4	5	9	8

B	9	4	4	5	8	9

C	6	8	4	8	7	9

D	8	4	2	5	9	8

E	4	1	3	8	7	7

5.

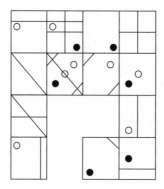

Which is the missing section?

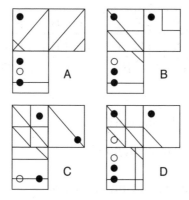

6.

A	G	D	K	G	R	K
F	R	N	L	A	B	D
L	B	B	F	F	N	N
K	N	R	A	L	D	B
D	D	G	G	K	K	R
N	K	A			L	G
B	L	F			F	A

Which is the missing section?

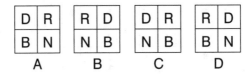

D	R
B	N

A

R	D
N	B

B

D	R
N	B

C

R	D
B	N

D

7.   Which is the odd one out?

secret, hat, dollar, coat, notch

8.   A marble statue is being carved by a sculptor. In the first week 35% is cut away, in the second week 20% of the remainder is cut away and in the third week 25% of the remainder is cut away and polished to produce the final statue. The weight of the final statue is 48.75 lbs. What was the weight of the original piece of marble?

Answer [   ]

9.

      & \$ * ? @ + # —— Ω & \$ * ? @ + # ——
Ω & \$ * ? @ + # —— Ω & ? @ + # ——
Ω & \$ * ? @ + # —— Ω

Which two symbols are missing?

      A & \$
      B * ?
      C \$ *
      D \$ &
      E * \$

10. Select two words that are synonyms, plus an antonym of these two synonyms, from the list of words below.

blessed, spurned, unlucky, refined, hapless, impolite, allied

11.

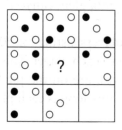

Draw the contents of the middle tile in accordance with the rules of logic already established.

12. Change the position of four words only in the sentence below in order for it to make complete sense.

The long flower bud splits and develops into an oval fruit that blooms open at maturity, revealing a mass of immature white hairs that cover the numerous seeds.

13. Which is the odd one out?

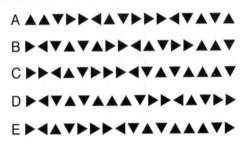

14. Identify two words (one from each set of brackets) that form a connection (analogy), thereby relating to the words in capitals in the same way.

DINGLE (corrie, dell, depression, abyss)

GULCH (wide, coomb, glen, canyon)

15. In a game of eight players lasting for 90 minutes, four reserves alternate equally with each player. This means that all players, including the reserves, are on the pitch for exactly the same length of time. For how long is each player on the pitch?

Answer _____

16. Insert numbers into the remaining blank squares so that the sums in each line and column are correct. All numbers to be inserted are less than 10.

	+		÷		=	3
×	■	−	■	×	■	+
	−		×	2	=	
÷	■	×		−	■	−
	−	3	+		=	
=	■	=	■	=	■	=
3	+		−		=	

17. Select two words that are synonyms, plus an antonym of these two synonyms, from the list of words below.

    keen, aromatic, synthetic, acrid, redolent, avid, natural

18.

Which two symbols are missing?

    A − −
    B − ▲
    C ▲▲
    D ▲ −
    E ▼▲

19. An electrical circuit wiring a set of four lights depends on a system of switches A, B, C and D. Each switch when working has the following effect on the lights:

Switch A turns lights 1 and 2 on/off or off/on

Switch B turns lights 2 and 4 on/off or off/on

Switch C turns lights 1 and 3 on/off or off/on

Switch D turns lights 3 and 4 on/off or off/on

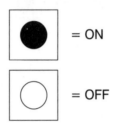

In the following, switches B A C D are thrown in turn, with the result that Figure 1 is transformed into Figure 2. One of the switches is therefore not working and has had no effect on the numbered lights.

Identify which one of the switches is not working.

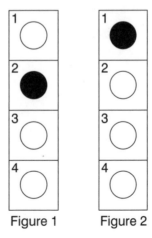

Figure 1   Figure 2

20.
$$9 \times ? = 7 \times \frac{405}{0.3125 \times 16}$$

Complete the equation by correctly identifying the missing part of the calculation from the list of options below.

a. $(45 \times \frac{7}{5})$ b. 4^3 c. $189 - 122$ d. $107.5 - 43.5$ e. $50 \times 120\%$

21. A   B   C   D   E   F   G   H

What letter is immediately to the right of the letter which comes four to the left of the letter that comes midway between the letter immediately to the right of the letter B and the letter immediately to the left of the letter H?

Answer [   ]

22. Which is the odd one out?

23. He worried that his business would inevitably suffer if nothing was done to relieve the burden of interest rates.

    One word has been removed from the passage above. Select that word from the choice below and reinstate it into its correct place in the passage.

    a. primary b. bank c. high d. money e. profit f. exchequer

24. A company produces 864 white, black and red motor vehicles per week in the ratio 1 : 5 : 3. How many black cars does the company produce per week?

    Answer [   ]

25. Which word in brackets is closest in meaning to the word in capitals?

    SANGUINE (pallid, wholesome, pious, sure, cheerful)

26. In the two numerical sequences below, one number that appears in the top sequence should appear in the bottom sequence and vice versa. Which two numbers should be changed round?

    88, 84, 70, 60

    97, 91, 82, 76

27.

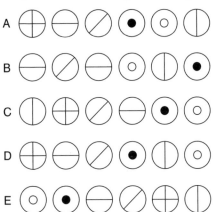

Which set of symbols should replace the question marks?

28. GERARD VARUNA is an anagram of which two words (4, 8 letters long) that are opposite in meaning?

Answer [   ]

29. Identify two words (one from each set of brackets) that form a connection (analogy), thereby relating to the words in capitals in the same way.

LETTUCE (flower, leaf, stalk, vegetable)

POTATO (root, pulse, jacket, tuber)

30. 10, 11, 13, 17, 25, ? , 73

What number should replace the question mark?

Answer [   ]

10

IQ Test Ten

Circle the answer(s), or write in the answer box provided.

1. Each set of nine numbers relates to the other in a certain way. Work out the logic behind the numbers in the left-hand box in order to determine which numbers are missing from the right-hand box.

12	21	6		28	?	14
27	3	15		63	?	35
18	9	24		42	21	?

Answer [ ]

2. Which word in brackets is most opposite in meaning to the word in capitals?

QUERULOUS (petulant, equable, worried, hopeful, straightforward)

3. Select two words that are synonyms, plus an antonym of these two synonyms, from the list of words below.

    flagrant, toneless, subtle, blemished, ornate, gracious, blatant

4. 5, 16, 49, ? , 445

    What number should replace the question mark?

    Answer [   ]

5. How tall is a sapling that is 3 feet shorter than a fence that is four times the height of the sapling?

    Answer [   ]

6.

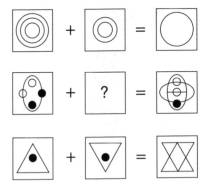

    Which is the missing square?

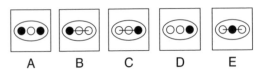

7. Identify two words (one from each set of brackets) that form a connection (analogy), thereby relating to the words in capitals in the same way.

   CIRCO- (globe, travel, around, circle)

   DEXTRO- (side, right, front, left)

8. In the two numerical sequences below, one number that appears in the top sequence should appear in the bottom sequence and vice versa. Which two numbers should be changed round?

   13, 20, 34, 60, 83

   12, 20, 36, 55, 92

9. Change the position of three words only in the sentence below in order for it to make complete sense.

   The magnificent city battlements, recently converted into promenades, command a surrounding view of the old alpine scenery.

10. ¾ ÷ ? = ?

    Complete the equation by correctly identifying the missing part of the calculation from the list of options below.

    a. 130%   b. $\dfrac{3 \times 2}{1.5 \times 3}$ c. $\dfrac{54}{50}$ d. 1.25   e. $\dfrac{270}{225}$

11. Select two words that are synonyms, plus an antonym of these two synonyms, from the list of words below.

    curious, pseudo, intrusive, spurious, spiritual, angry, authentic

12. In a right-angled triangle what is the length of the hypotenuse if the two shortest sides are 10 and 24 cm respectively?

                                    Answer [   ]

13.

‖& ▲ §β♀♫‖& ▲ §β♀♫‖& ▲ §β‖&
▲ §β♀♫& ▲ §β♀♫‖& ▲ §β♀♫& ▲ §
β♀♫

Which two symbols are missing?

                A ▲ §
                B ♀ ♫
                C § β
                D & ▲
                E & ▲

14. An electrical circuit wiring a set of four lights depends on a system of switches A, B, C and D. Each switch when working has the following effect on the lights:

Switch A turns lights 1 and 2 on/off or off/on

Switch B turns lights 2 and 4 on/off or off/on

Switch C turns lights 1 and 3 on/off or off/on

Switch D turns lights 3 and 4 on/off or off/on

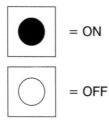

= ON

= OFF

In the following, switches D B A C are thrown in turn, with the result that Figure 1 is transformed into Figure 2. One of the switches is therefore not working and has had no effect on the numbered lights.

Identify which one of the switches is not working.

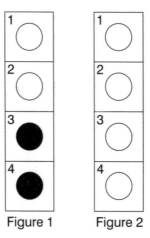

Figure 1   Figure 2

15.

Which of the figures below, when rotated correctly, is a mirror-image of the figure above?

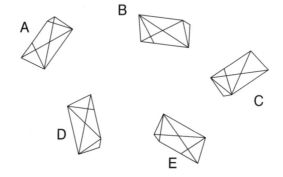

16. I have collected 253 strawberries which I want to put into punnets for handing out to my neighbours. All punnets must contain the same number of strawberries and I wish to use as few punnets as possible. How many of my neighbours received a punnet of strawberries, and how many strawberries did each punnet contain?

Answer [   ]

17. Which is the odd one out?

pivotal, incidental, substantive, seminal, salient

18. Insert the numbers listed into the circles so that – for any
    particular circle – the sum of the numbers in the circles
    connected to it equals the value corresponding to that circled
    number in the list. For example:

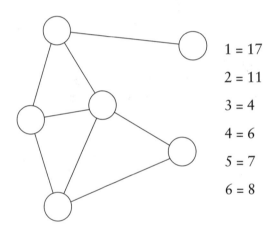

1 = 14 (4 + 7 + 3)

3 = 1

4 = 8 (1 + 7)

7 = 5 (1 + 4)

1 = 17

2 = 11

3 = 4

4 = 6

5 = 7

6 = 8

19. LIGAMENT, MARKSMAN , ? , ELEGANCE, AGITATED

Which word is missing?

KINETICS, SKELETAL, MONASTIC, GLOSSARY,
SPECIMEN

20.

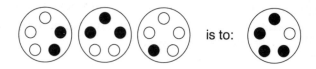

as:

is to:

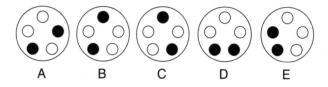

is to:

21. Which of the following is not an anagram of a type of fish?

SO URGENT

ODD HACK

THE LANDS

SANDIER

FIT CASH

UNFOLDER

22. $\dfrac{(39+56)}{60\%} = ? \times 3$

Complete the equation by correctly identifying the missing part of the calculation from the list of options below.

a. $\dfrac{273}{7}$ b. $\dfrac{245}{7^2}$ c. $\dfrac{133}{7}$ d. $5^2 - 7$ e. $4^2 + 5$

23. Which two words are closest in meaning?

trivial, idiomatic, abject, foolish, vernacular, lively

24. What is the value of $-12 + -15$?

Answer [ ]

25. A   B   C   D   E   F   G   H

What letter is three to the right of the letter immediately to the left of the letter three to the left of the letter two to the right of the letter F ?

Answer [ ]

26.

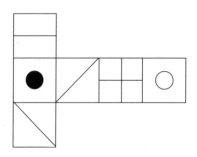

When the above is folded to form a cube, just two of the following can be produced. Which two?

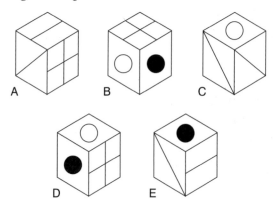

27. Melt a teaspoonful of butter in the pan, add the cake mixture, and stir over a medium heat.

One word has been removed from the passage above. Select that word from the choice below and reinstate it into its correct place in the passage.

a. oven b. frying c. powder d. briskly e. slow f. soft

28. Identify two words (one from each set of brackets) that form a connection (analogy), thereby relating to the words in capitals in the same way.

CORNET (brass, horn, trumpet, wind)

FIFE (woodwind, drum, clarinet, flute)

29.   12348   is to   32418

    and   12489   is to   84129

    and   24567   is to   57624

    therefore   12789   is to   ?

                                    Answer [   ]

30. By making a single cut, divide the shape into two identical (size and shape) pieces.

11

IQ Test Eleven

Circle the answer(s), or write in the answer box provided.

1. Which word in brackets is closest in meaning to the word in capitals?

   MAGNILOQUENT (exalted, enlarged, gifted, favoured, hypnotic)

2. Which is the odd one out?

   A Σ ↕⊢FK¶ §£ & $♀◙

   B K⊢Σ §♀&◙ $£ ¶ F↕

   C F§◙$⊢K↕&Σ ¶£♀

   D ◙♀↕£⊢$ K ¶Σ §F£

   E &◙F♀§↕ Σ£¶⊢K$

3. A company hires a fleet of buses to transport its workforce to a conference. If 689 workers attended the conference, and each bus seats 35 passengers, how many buses are required?

   Answer [   ]

4. Only one group of six letters below can be rearranged to spell out a six-letter word in the English language. Identify the word.

BEOPLA

ICKTEA

WLONUD

XOLEIN

ARHCLO

HATOND

INMETL

5.

$$0.85 \times 220 = \frac{?}{25\% \times 20}$$

Complete the equation by correctly identifying the missing part of the calculation from the list of options below.

a. $1090 - 145$ b. 935 c. $85 + 29^2$ d. $31^2 - 28$ e. 945

6.   Which is the odd one out?

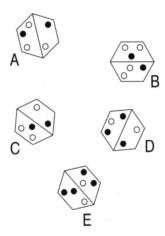

7.   Select two words that are synonyms, plus an antonym of these two synonyms, from the list of words below.

foolish, lavish, welcome, manifest, laughable, vague, abstruse

8. An electrical circuit wiring a set of four lights depends on a system of switches A, B, C and D. Each switch when working has the following effect on the lights:

Switch A turns lights 1 and 2 on/off or off/on

Switch B turns lights 2 and 4 on/off or off/on

Switch C turns lights 1 and 3 on/off or off/on

Switch D turns lights 3 and 4 on/off or off/on

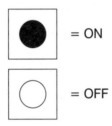

In the following, switches D A B C are thrown in turn, with the result that Figure 1 is transformed into Figure 2. One of the switches is therefore not working and has had no effect on the numbered lights.

Identify which one of the switches is not working.

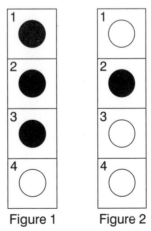

Figure 1   Figure 2

9.

Z		W	T
W	V		Q
U	T		O
T		Q	N

Which is the missing section?

 A

 B

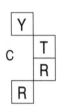 C

D

10. Which four-figure number contains four different digits and meets the following criteria? The first digit is twice the value of the fourth digit and two more than the second digit. The third digit is one more than the first digit and four more than the fourth digit.

Answer [ ]

11. Change the position of four words only in the sentence below in order for it to make complete sense.

Given this e-mail if you do not want to use the user name deselect here as an option name.

12. 100, 93, 79, 58, ?

What number should replace the question mark?

Answer [ ]

13. Which is the odd one out?

panther, jaguar, jackal, tiger, puma

14.

3	6	9	4	8	2		2	9	7	9	5	6
7	3	8	9	6	4		?	?	?	?	?	?

The top set of six numbers has a relationship to the set of six numbers below. The two sets of six boxes on the left have the same relationship as the two sets of six boxes on the right. Which set of numbers should therefore replace the question marks?

A | 5 | 9 | 5 | 9 | 1 | 2 |

B | 5 | 6 | 4 | 6 | 3 | 13 |

C | 6 | 10 | 5 | 9 | 2 | 1 |

D | 5 | 9 | 1 | 2 | 5 | 9 |

E | 5 | 7 | 5 | 9 | 1 | 2 |

15.

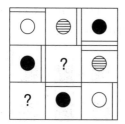

Which are the two missing squares?

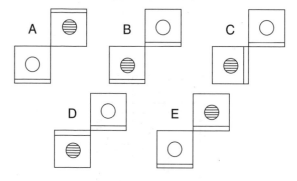

16. By adopting a more consensual leadership style than his, he sought to restore party unity on integration with Europe and other issues.

One word has been removed from the passage above. Select that word from the choice below and reinstate it into its correct place in the passage.

a. flagging b. successive c. predecessor d. urgent e. colleague f. Western

17. Insert numbers into the remaining blank squares so that the sums in each line and column are correct. All numbers to be inserted are less than 10.

	×		−		=	9
+	■	+	■	−	■	−
	−		×	4	=	
−	■	−	■	×	■	×
	−	5	+		=	
=	■	=	■	=	■	=
1	×		÷		=	

18.

Draw the contents of the middle tile in accordance with the rules of logic already established.

19. Select two words that are synonyms, plus an antonym of these two synonyms, from the list of words below.

attentive, profane, abrupt, brazen, wise, fearful, offhand

20. A photograph measuring 3.9 × 4.6 cm is to be enlarged. If the shortest side of the enlargement is 17.55 cm, what is the length of the longest side?

Answer [   ]

21. Identify two words (one from each set of brackets) that form a connection (analogy), thereby relating to the words in capitals in the same way.

PASCAL (speed, frequency, pressure, current)

NEWTON (force, power, heat, energy)

22. In the two numerical sequences below, one number that appears in the top sequence should appear in the bottom sequence and vice versa. Which two numbers should be changed round?

12, 14, 18, 22, 32, 34, 38

13, 16, 26, 24, 28, 36, 42

23.

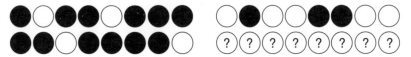

Which set of diagrams below should replace the question marks?

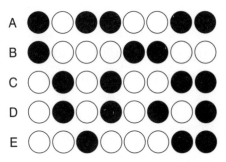

24. Identify two words (one from each set of brackets) that form a connection (analogy), thereby relating to the words in capitals in the same way.

    DIAGONAL (opposite, oblique, adjacent, direction)

    CROSSWISE (transverse, path, course, vertices)

25.

    Which symbol is missing?

    A ▲
    B ◀
    C ▼
    D ▶

26. A   B   C   D   E   F   G   H

    What letter is three to the left of the letter immediately to the right of the letter which is four to the right of the letter B ?

    Answer [   ]

27. In 15 years' time the combined age of my four brothers will be 107. What will it be in six years' time?

    Answer [   ]

28. Which word in brackets is most opposite in meaning to the word in capitals?

    DECADENT (overjoyed, clean, ethical, immodest, relaxed)

29.

$$? + \frac{96 + 57}{9} = 18^2 - \frac{1038}{2(\sqrt{9})}$$

Complete the equation by correctly identifying the missing part of the calculation from the list of options below.

a. $\dfrac{67 \times 36}{77 - 59}$ b. $12^2 + 12$ c. $11^2 + \dfrac{45}{3}$ d. $\dfrac{16^2}{2}$ e. $\dfrac{96}{0.75}$

30.

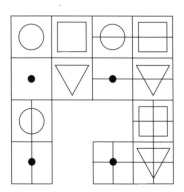

Which is the missing section?

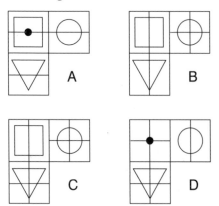

IQ Test Twelve

Circle the answer(s), or write in the answer box provided.

1. What is −4 − +13 ?

    Answer [   ]

2. Identify two words (one from each set of brackets) that form a connection (analogy), thereby relating to the words in capitals in the same way.

    TEMPO (sound, short, volume, speed)

    CRESCENDO (vigour, increase, scale, speed)

3. $\dfrac{8 \times 4 \times 6}{?} = \dfrac{4 \times 11 \times 2 \times 2 \times 5.5}{11^2 \times 0.5}$

    Complete the equation by correctly identifying the missing part of the calculation from the list of options below.

    a. $2^3 + 5$ b. $\dfrac{144}{12} + 2$ c. $3^2 + 5$ d. $\dfrac{24}{3}$ e. $2^2 \times 3$

4.

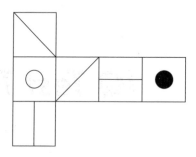

When the above is folded to form a cube, just two of the following can be produced. Which two?

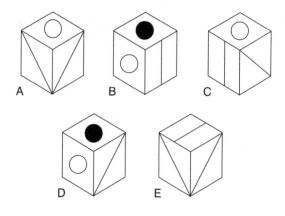

5. Which word in brackets is most opposite in meaning to the word in capitals?

ABASHED (confident, occupied, active, durable, absolved)

6.

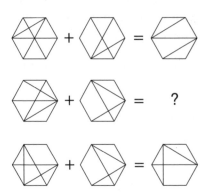

Which hexagon below should replace the question mark?

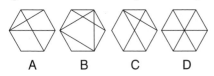

    A   B   C   D

7.   10, 50, 13, 45, 18, 38, ?, ?

What two numbers should replace the question marks?

Answer [   ]

8. A B C D E F G H

What letter is two to the right of the letter which comes five to the left of the letter that comes two to the right of the letter which is three to the left of the letter H?

Answer [   ]

9. An electrical circuit wiring a set of four lights depends on a system of switches A, B, C and D. Each switch when working has the following effect on the lights:

Switch A turns lights 1 and 2 on/off or off/on

Switch B turns lights 2 and 4 on/off or off/on

Switch C turns lights 1 and 3 on/off or off/on

Switch D turns lights 3 and 4 on/off or off/on

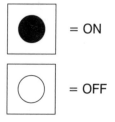

In the following, switches A C D B are thrown in turn, with the result that Figure 1 is transformed into Figure 2. One of the switches is therefore not working and has had no effect on the numbered lights.

Identify which one of the switches is not working.

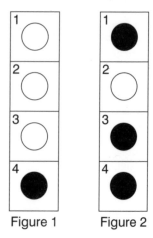

Figure 1   Figure 2

10.

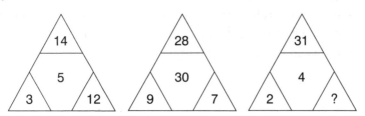

What number should replace the question mark?

Answer [   ]

11. Cuttlefish have some importance, not only for their flesh, which is eaten in many countries, but also for the bone of their shell and for the ink they eject to cloud the water as protection from their enemies.

One word has been removed from the passage above. Select that word from the choice below and reinstate it into its correct place in the passage.

a. edible b. soft c. brown d. economic e. surprising f. foreign

12. Which two words are closest in meaning?

effects, parameter, section, criterion, periphery, view

13. Insert the numbers listed into the circles so that – for any particular circle – the sum of the numbers in the circles connected to it equals the value corresponding to that circled number in the list. For example:

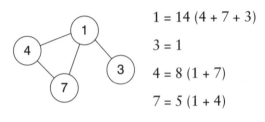

1 = 14 (4 + 7 + 3)

3 = 1

4 = 8 (1 + 7)

7 = 5 (1 + 4)

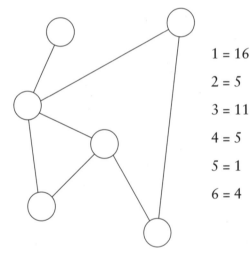

1 = 16

2 = 5

3 = 11

4 = 5

5 = 1

6 = 4

14.

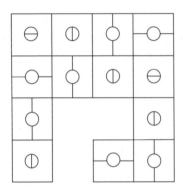

Which is the missing section?

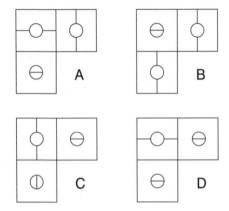

15. Select two words that are synonyms, plus an antonym of these two synonyms, from the list of words below.

grateful, blithe, unkind, buoyant, morose, relieved, worried

16.

'Ω Χ Η Σ Μ Ψ • 'Ω Χ Η Σ Μ Ψ ○ 'Ω Χ Η Σ
Μ Ψ • • 'Ω Χ Η Σ Μ Ψ ○ ○ 'Ω Χ Η Σ Μ • •
'Ω Χ Η Σ Μ Ψ ○ ○ ○

Which two symbols are missing?

A • 'Ω
B ○ 'Ω
C 'Ω Χ
D Ψ •
E • Ψ

17. Select two words that are synonyms, plus an antonym of these two synonyms, from the list of words below.

fatuous, inanimate, worthwhile, stifled, active, indisposed, inert

18. 12, 34, 10, 11, 12, 5, 6 ,7, 13, 14, ?, ?

Logically, what two numbers should replace the question marks?

Answer [   ]

19. may, rid, bar, sea, ???, den, row, led

What word is missing?

can, pan, pot, hem, leg

20. In a consignment of eggs 552 were cracked, which was 12 per cent of the total consignment.

    How many eggs were in the consignment?

    Answer [   ]

21. Change the position of five words only in the sentence below in order for it to make complete sense.

    The domesticated peafowl has been feral in many parts of the Pacific but there are common populations in some world islands.

22. $$\frac{1053 \div 13}{60\% \times 90} = \frac{?}{96}$$

    Complete the equation by correctly identifying the missing part of the calculation from the list of options below.

    a. 168   b. 144   c. 132   d. $\sqrt{196} \times 7$ e. 13^2

23. Use every letter of the phrase THE RAVENOUS BAD PLAGUE once each only to spell out the names of three world rivers.

    _____

24. Which is the odd one out?

    lax, torpid, remiss, lackadaisical, insouciant

25. In the two numerical sequences below, one number that appears in the top sequence should appear in the bottom sequence and vice versa. Which two numbers should be changed round?

   0.75, 3, 5.25, 6.75, 9.75

   1.25, 4, 7.5, 9.5, 12.25

26. Which does not belong in this sequence?

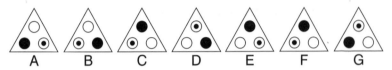

27.

4		3	5
7	9		8
5			6
8	10	7	9

   Which is the missing section?

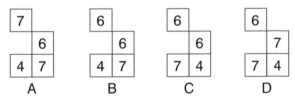

28. Identify two words (one from each set of brackets) that form a connection (analogy), thereby relating to the words in capitals in the same way.

   PIE (chart, circle, meat, loop)

   BAR (rod, section, column, coordinate)

29. The numbers in each set of nine relate to each other in a certain way. Work out the logic behind the numbers in the left-hand box in order to determine which number is missing from the right-hand box.

4	10	8		9	3	?
11	2	13		15	6	15
5	4	7		8	3	11

Answer [   ]

30.

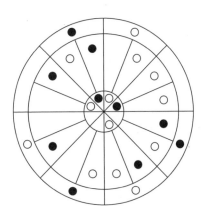

Complete the pattern in accordance with the rules of logic already established.

Answers, explanations and assessment

Answers to IQ Test One

1. A; each line moves 45° clockwise from top to bottom.

2. Synonyms: thrive, burgeon
   Antonym: wither

3. 22 and 24: there are two interwoven sequences. Starting at 19, alternate numbers progress +2, +3, +4, +5. Starting at 20, alternate numbers progress +2, +4, +6, +8.

4. d, conserved: The institution houses collections of objects of artistic, historic and scientific interest, **conserved** and displayed for the edification and enjoyment of the public.

5. dispersion: it means scattering, the rest are gathering.

6. d

7. 47632: all the others are three-digit numbers followed by their square root, eg 361 followed by its square root, 19.

8. parade, somnambulate. The keyword to insert is walk: parade on a cat-walk, sleepwalk is to somnambulate.

9. irreverent

10. 69237

   A B C D E   E C B D A
   1 2 5 9 3   3 5 2 9 1
   7 2 9 3 6   6 9 2 3 7

11. e. 0.25

12.

Each line of three tiles across and down contains a line in the top corner, a line in the middle, a line in the bottom corner and a black dot.

13.

9	÷	3	×	2	=	6
+	■	−	■	×	■	+
6	+	1	−	4	=	3
÷	■	+	■	−	■	÷
3	×	3	−	6	=	3
=	■	=	■	=	■	=
5	÷	5	+	2	=	3

14. landrace, calendar

15. KP: there are two alternate sequences. Starting at A, ABcDefGhijK; starting at Z, ZYxWvuTsrqP.

16. E: each number on the bottom line is the sum of the digits of the number directly above it.

17. 8: 112 pairs of shoes = 224 shoes. 224 ÷ 28 = 8.

18. C: A and B are the same string, albeit starting in a different position, as are D and E.

19. 2.5 and 3. In the top sequence the numbers progress × 1.5. In the bottom sequence the numbers progress × 2.5.

20. B: looking across and down the contents of the first two tiles are combined to produce the contents of the end tile.

21. anterior, obverse

22. If you are printing on glossy *media* or transparencies, place a support *sheet*, or a sheet of plain *paper*, beneath the *stack*, or load only one sheet at a time.

23. d

24. derivative, archetypal

25. Synonyms: excuse, condone
    Antonym: condemn

26. D: the rest are the same figure rotated.

27. 1 apple costs £0.18 and 1 banana costs £0.14.

28. Switch C is faulty.

29. A: each line across and down contains one each of the lines in a different position (the lines are moving downwards one notch at a time; when they reach the bottom they return to the top position at the next stage).

30. Data processing is used for a wide variety of applications, including the processing of seismic data for oil and mineral exploration, the analysis of new product designs, the processing of satellite imagery, and the analysis of data from scientific experiments.

Assessment

Scores between:	Rating
27–30	Very highly exceptional
24–26	High expert
21–23	Expert
19–20	Very high average
17–18	High average
13–16	Middle average
10–12	Low average
6–9	Borderline low
3–5	Low
0–2	Very low

Answers to IQ Test Two

1. D: looking across, numbers in each line progress +1, –2, +3, –4; looking down, numbers progress –4, +3, –2, +1.

2. Switch B is faulty.

3. WNW, WSW, SSW, SSE, SE, ESE, ENE, NNE

4.

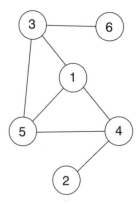

5. barren

6. Synonyms: spearhead, vanguard
    Antonym: stern

7. D: columns 1 and 3 are the same symbols reversed, as are columns 2 and 4.

8. clarinet, harp, trumpet

9. 61 and 63 should be reversed. The first sequence progresses
    –11, –13, –15, –17, –19. The second sequence progresses
    –12, –14, –16, –18, –20.

10. fedora: the rest are a sequence where the first two letters are
    also the first two letters of the months March, April, May,
    June, July, August.

11.

    Each line across and down contains a circle of each size and a
    black dot.

12. 34826: each number is the sum of the last two digits of the
    previous number, preceded by the remaining numbers in
    reverse.

13. *Sap* rises from the *root* of the maple tree in the form of crude
    sap, a solution of *material* that is absorbed from the *soil*.

14. 18.6, 37.6. There are two interwoven sequences: starting at 45
    alternate numbers are –3.7. Starting at 4 alternate numbers
    are +7.3.

15. back, leg

16. a

17. Synonyms: practicable, feasible
    Antonym: impossible

18. B: in the others the long hand moves 45° clockwise and the short hand moves 90° clockwise.

19. C: the water flows fastest at the narrowest point.

20. A

21. H

22. a

23. masticate, gnaw

24. B: ignore black symbols as they are not carried forward to the final circle. All white symbols are carried forward; however, circles change to squares and vice versa.

25. 18: multiply the bottom numbers to obtain the numbers at the top, albeit they are at the top of a different pyramid.

26.

$$1\frac{23}{27} \qquad \frac{25}{4} \div \frac{27}{8} = \frac{25}{4} \times \frac{8}{27}$$

27. f, bleak: It is a largely agricultural country of varied scenery from **bleak** moorland, loughs and islands to the beautiful coastline around West Bay.

28. 13: in each line multiply the first and last numbers, then add 1 to obtain the middle number.

29. skin, hair

30.

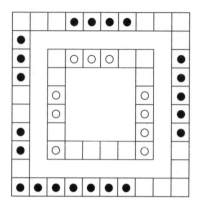

In each square, start at the bottom left-hand square, and working clockwise, place one circle, then miss one square and place two circles, then miss two squares and place three circles, etc.

Assessment

Scores between:	Rating
27–30	Very highly exceptional
24–26	High expert
21–23	Expert
19–20	Very high average
17–18	High average
13–16	Middle average
10–12	Low average
6–9	Borderline low
3–5	Low
0–2	Very low

Answers to IQ Test Three

1. 6: looking down columns, the number formed by the three digits in column one plus the number formed by the three digits in column two, equals the number formed in column three. For example; 394 + 568 = 962.

2. Because *shelter* is necessary for everyone, the problem of providing adequate *housing* has long been a concern, not only of *individuals* but also of governments.

3. Tuesday

4. Synonyms: prosaic, mundane
   Antonym: fascinating

5. 11: the rule is replace – – with +, so –26 + 37 = 11.

6. A: lines from the first two boxes are carried forward to the third box, except when two lines appear in the same position, in which case they are cancelled out.

7. able, end. Each of these words can be preceded with the words in capitals: **par**able and **leg**end.

8

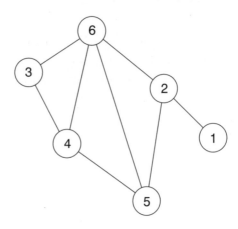

9.   c, 17.25

10. Switch B is faulty.

11. 86213579: arrange the even digits in descending order followed by the odd digits in ascending order.

12. dry, set: paint dries, concrete sets.

13. A: the square increases in size and goes in the middle, the circle increases in size and goes at the bottom and the rectangle rotates 90° and goes at the top.

14. 16 and 18 need to be exchanged. The top sequence progresses +21, +24, +27, +30. The bottom sequence progresses +20, +24, +28, +32.

15. e, legally: Although he did not enter the bank, he drove the getaway car, which **legally** makes him an accessory before the fact.

16. D

17. corporal, physical

18. Milly £620   Tilly £220
    Milly 620 – 60 = 560   Milly 620 + 10 = 630
    Tilly 220 + 60 = 280   Tilly 220 – 10 = 210

19. B and C

20. 6: the sequence progresses –0, –1, –2 repeated.

21. Synonyms: proscribe, boycott
    Antonym: sanction

22. a, 2132

23. simple: the rest have alternate consonant/vowel arrangement.

24. 1: multiply the bottom two numbers then take the square root, ie 1 × 4 = 4 and $\sqrt{4}$ = 2.

25. C

26. Gordon 64 and Tony 48: when Gordon was 48, Tony was 32 (ie half the age Gordon is now).

27. cabbage, broccoli, beans

28. implement

29. IX   VII   IV   III   XI

30. C D B

Assessment

Scores between:	Rating
27–30	Very highly exceptional
24–26	High expert
21–23	Expert
19–20	Very high average
17–18	High average
13–16	Middle average
10–12	Low average
6–9	Borderline low
3–5	Low
0–2	Very low

Answers to IQ Test Four

1. opinion, viewpoint

2. b. 698 : 62. $(6 \times 9) + 8 = 62$.

3. D

4. restrain: here/rely, host/star, aura/rank, coin/inch

5. a

6. b

7.
    $\dfrac{13}{28}$ Change fractions to the lowest common denominator:

    $\dfrac{12}{28}$ $\dfrac{13}{28}$ $\dfrac{10}{28}$

8. frantic, heedless

9. B: in lines across the dot moves one corner clockwise and alternates black/white. In columns down the dot moves one corner anti-clockwise and alternates black/white.

10. Synonyms: weaken, debilitate
    Antonym: invigorate

11. d

12. *Popular* in the Middle Ages, a Bestiary is a type of book that purports to describe all the animals in creation, real or *imaginary*, and the *human* traits they exemplify.

13. 10 lb: 50/5 = 10.

14. sealed

15.

Looking across, lines move 45° clockwise. Looking down, lines move 45° anti-clockwise.

16. 15 and 23 should be exchanged. Both sequences progress × 2 + 1.

17. F

18. 47 minutes. 12 noon less 47 minutes = 11.13. 11.13 less 1 hour 39 minutes = 9.34. 8 am plus 94 minutes (47 × 2) = 9.34.

19. rich

20. E: the black dot is moving one corner clockwise at each stage and the white dot is moving one corner anti-clockwise at each stage.

21. Synonyms: tractable, willing
    Antonym: obstinate

22. 10: each diagonal line of numbers, starting with the top left-hand corner number, increases by 1 each time, ie:

4

2 + 3 = 5

2 + 1 + 3 = 6

2 + 1 + 2 + 2 =7

4 + 1 + 3 = 8

5 + 4 = 9

10

23. casino: all the other words form a sequence where each word commences with the middle two letters of the previous word.

24.

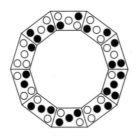

Opposite segments have the same arrangement of dots, but with black/white reversal.

25. B: all the even numbers are divided by 2 and all the odd numbers are multiplied by 2.

26. d, prospective: The shop is a delight to **prospective** travellers as it is prepared to outfit anyone for anything, from a walk in the country to an African safari or an Arctic expedition.

27. Switch C is faulty.

28. 42: the sequence progresses +6, +12, +18, +24, +30.

29. gather, protect

30. B: all black dots change to a horizontal line, all white dots are unaffected.

Assessment

Scores between:	Rating
27–30	Very highly exceptional
24–26	High expert
21–23	Expert
19–20	Very high average
17–18	High average
13–16	Middle average
10–12	Low average
6–9	Borderline low
3–5	Low
0–2	Very low

Answers to IQ Test Five

1. B: a contains the same symbols as D in reverse and C contains the same symbols as E in reverse.

2. 15: $(6 \times 10) \div 4$.

3. Switch D is faulty.

4. −1 and −2: the sequence progresses +1, −2, +3, −4, +5, −6.

5. whimsical, eerie

6. Synonyms: console, assuage
    Antonym: torment

7. 14.5 and 13.5 should be interchanged. The top sequence progresses +3, +3.5, +4, +4.5, +5. The bottom sequence progresses +5, +4.5, +4, +3.5.

8. irritation

9.

Looking across and down, all lines and symbols from the first two tiles are carried forward to the third tile, except when the same line or symbol appears in both the first two tiles, in which case they are cancelled out.

10. 137: add the three surrounding numbers in the position as in the examples below:

1	2	6	12	28	58
3	6	10	28	51	137

$1 + 2 + 3 = 6$ $6 + 12 + 10 = 28$ $28 + 58 + 51 = 137$

11. IFCLEA = facile

12. c

13. virtuous, nefarious

14. D: the first three circles change places with the last three circles.

15. If customers like the goods, the *trademark* enables them to *know* what to look for in the *future*; if they *dislike* the *product*, they will avoid goods with that trademark.

16.

5	×	2	−	6	=	4
+	■	+	■	×	■	+
2	×	8	÷	4	=	4
−	■	÷	■	÷	■	÷
3	+	5	−	6	=	2
=	■	=	■	=	■	=
4	×	2	−	4	=	4

17. anodyne: it is weak, the rest are powerful.

18. B: in each line both across and down, one of the three rings is black.

19. 11

    3 numbers 29 × 3 = 87 total

    2 numbers 38 × 2 = 76 total

    The third number must therefore be 87 – 76 = 11.

20. c, harmful: A relatively thin envelope, the atmosphere consists of layers of gases that support life and provide protection from **harmful** radiation.

21. B

22. Public companies can sell their shares to the general public, whereas private companies cannot sell shares to, or raise money from, the general public.

23. B: the top numbers move to the same bottom positions as in the first set.

24. goose, crow

25. B: the third line is the first line in reverse, and the fourth line is the second line in reverse.

26. 4254: the centre number in each row is the product of the digits on the left, followed by the product of the digits on the right, ie 7 × 2 × 3 = 42 and 6 × 3 × 3 = 54.

27. HIRX: the first three letters move four places forward in the alphabet, while the fourth letter moves forward five places.

28. b

29. Synonyms: brackish, undrinkable

   Antonym: unpolluted

30. E: the second five symbols are a mirror image of the first five symbols.

Assessment

Scores between:	Rating
27–30	Very highly exceptional
24–26	High expert
21–23	Expert
19–20	Very high average
17–18	High average
13–16	Middle average
10–12	Low average
6–9	Borderline low
3–5	Low
0–2	Very low

Answers to IQ Test Six

1. F

2. 16 cm

$$65 \text{ cm}^2 = 4225$$

$$\text{less} \quad 63 \text{ cm}^2 = \frac{3969}{256}$$

$$\sqrt{256} = 16 \text{ (Pythagoras)}$$

3. 453: in each pyramid divide the top number by 2, the bottom left number by 3 and the bottom right number by 4, to produce the three digits in the middle.

4. B: the top left symbol moves to bottom left, the top right symbol moves to bottom right, the bottom left symbol moves to top right and the bottom right symbol moves to top left.

5. Harry 32, Larry 56, Carrie 63.

6. Like the *rhythms* which occur in *nature*, such as the *motion* of the planets, the succession of *seasons*, and the beating of the *heart*, musical rhythm is usually organized in regular recurring *patterns*.

7. 2918: add the first four numbers, ie 7 + 9 + 5 + 8 = 29; followed by the last three numbers, ie 2 + 7 + 9 = 18.

8. 6: the number formed by the top three digits when added to the number formed by the bottom three digits equals the number formed by the middle three digits.

9. gallery: it is the part of the theatre for the audience. The rest are stages or part of the stage for the performers.

10. C: the rest are the same figure rotated.

11. 7 2 3

    4 6 8

    2 1 5

    Subtract 1 from each figure. The first column then becomes the top line, the second column becomes the middle line and the third column becomes the bottom line.

12. Synonyms: gracious, charitable

    Antonym: impolite

13. b, 120 (5 × 4 × 3 × 2 × 1).

14. access, egress

15. D: B is the same as C and A is the same as E.

16. e

17. 180 and 120 should be interchanged. The top sequence progresses ×2, ×3, ×2, ×3, ×2. The bottom sequence progresses ×3, ×2, ×3, ×2, ×3.

18. farcical, risible

19. real madam = marmalade. The fruits are apricot (rip coat), avocado (ova coda), blueberry (burly beer), pineapple (pipe panel), watermelon (alert women) and grapefruit (part figure).

20. 24: ¼ or 4 out of 16 took sugar only. ⅝ or 10 out of 16 took milk and sugar. 1 out of 16 took milk only. The remainder, ie 1 out of 16 took it black. 384 ÷ 16 = 24.

21. b, whorls: The stiff, intricate branches form **whorls** around the trunk and are covered with overlapping, scale-shaped leaves.

22. 63: the sequence progresses +14, +15, +16, +17.

23. Synonyms: variable, flexible
    Antonym: firm

24.

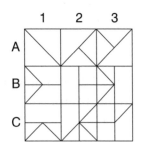

Tile 3C is incorrect and should be replaced by tile C.

25. RHYTHM: the penultimate letter of each word is in the alphabetic sequence A B C D E F G H.

26.

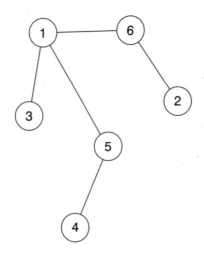

27. oxymoron, tautology

28. C: from top to bottom all the symbols move on one place (the end symbol moves to the front).

29. Switch A is faulty.

30.

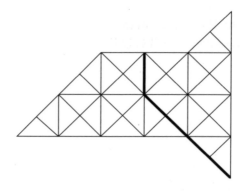

Assessment

Scores between:	Rating
27–30	Very highly exceptional
24–26	High expert
21–23	Expert
19–20	Very high average
17–18	High average
13–16	Middle average
10–12	Low average
6–9	Borderline low
3–5	Low
0–2	Very low

Answers to IQ Test Seven

1. 1:

$$\frac{30}{45} = \frac{6}{9} \times 144 = 96$$

$$\frac{19}{57} = \frac{1}{3} \times \ 96 = 32$$

$$12.5\% \times 32 \ = 4$$

$$\frac{1}{4} \times 4 \qquad = 1$$

2. copper, argon, radium

3. 35%. First stall 16 out of 64 = 25%. Second stall 36 out of 60 = 60%. Difference in percentages = 35%.

4. Synonyms: contrary, recalcitrant
    Antonym: compliant

5. b

6. D

7. B

8. e, literary: Her novels reflect her background, highly allusive and **literary** in style, they draw their characters from academic and artistic works.

9. 0.6875

$$\frac{6}{16} + \frac{5}{16} = \frac{11}{16} = 0.6875$$

10. Synonyms: miscellaneous, assorted

    Antonym: uniform

11. 97.4: the sequence progresses −0.2, −0.6, −1.8, −5.4, −16.2 (ie multiplying the difference by 3 each time).

12. D: in each line take the difference between the numbers of black and white dots respectively to arrive at the number and colour of dots in the final square.

13. artichoke

14. realigns: the remaining words are all anagrams.

15. 37: the rule is to replace + − with −. Thus 56 − 19 = 37.

16. seditious, mutinous

17.

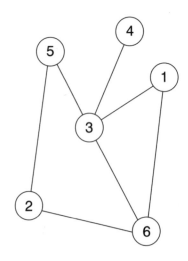

18. A: looking down, the number of lines increases by 1 each time. Looking across, the number of lines also increases by 1, but the lines alternate horizontally and vertically.

19. d

20. wealthy, priesthood

21. C

22. neo-, palaeo-

23. 62 and 59 should be interchanged. The top sequence progresses +17, +18, +19, +20. The bottom sequence progresses +18, +16, +14, +12.

24. A and E

25. Peacekeeping has always been conducted with the *consent* of the disputants, who at the very least agree to *attempt* to settle their *differences* and not endanger the *safety* of the peacekeeping forces.

26. 27: in the first row divide every number by 7 to obtain the digits in the brackets; in the second row divide by 8, and in the third row divide by 9.

27. concave

28. 4: looking across each line, add the first two numbers, then add 1 to the total to obtain the third number, ie (2 + 3) + 1 = 6.

29. Switch A is faulty.

30. A B D

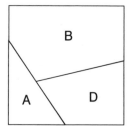

Assessment

Scores between:	Rating
27–30	Very highly exceptional
24–26	High expert
21–23	Expert
19–20	Very high average
17–18	High average
13–16	Middle average
10–12	Low average
6–9	Borderline low
3–5	Low
0–2	Very low

Answers to IQ Test Eight

1. f, generally: The metal is **generally** in the form of a bar, either straight, or bent into the shape of a horseshoe.

2. 55°: as the two right-hand triangles are identical, angle Y is 35°. Angle W is therefore 180 – (90 + 35) = 55 as angle Z is 90° (a right angle) and the three angles in a triangle always total 180°. As angles W and X are identical, the answer is therefore 55°.

3. hypotenuse, diameter

4. C: add 3 to the first, third and fifth numbers. Add 4 to the second, fourth and sixth numbers.

5. E: the cross in the middle is extracted and the figures originally contained in the rectangle attach themselves to the end of the nearest arm of the cross anti-clockwise.

6. A partnership is a business association of two or more people who have formally agreed to work together, each contributing skills, labour and resources to the venture in return for a pre-arranged share of the profits.

7. 8: in each row multiply the first and third digits to obtain the number formed by the second and fourth digits.

8. Synonyms: wearisome, tiresome
    Antonym: exhilarating

9. e

10.

Looking both across and down, the contents of the first two tiles are merged to produce the contents of the third tile.

11. Switch D is faulty.

12. c. 8278 : 1510 : 25

$8 + 7 = 15$; $2 + 8 = 10$ 1510

$1 + 1 = 2$; $5 + 0 = 5$ 25

13. D: the others are in the same order, albeit starting at a different symbol.

14. pithy, garrulous

15. d

16. avoid

17. D

18. Instead of actively *transmitting* radio signals, some of the first communication *satellites* had no radio *equipment* aboard and were designed to operate in a *passive* mode.

19. A: B is the same as G; C is the same as E; D is the same as F.

20. ordinate, rationed

21. 70: the sequence progresses −18, −17, −18, −17.

22. institute: it means to found. The rest mean to recall or annul.

23. a

24. C: the black symbols have a horizontal line added. The white symbols change to black.

25. ABDGKP: ABcDefGhijKlmnoP.

26. 24 cm and 32 cm (Pythagoras).

$$40 \text{ cm}^2 = 1600 \qquad 24^2 = 576$$
$$32^2 = \underline{1024}$$
$$1600$$

27. hand, heart

28. Synonyms: engaging, arresting

Antonym: unremarkable

29. 45 and 47 should be interchanged. The top sequence progresses –20, –21, –22, –23, –24. The bottom sequence progresses –21, –22, –23, –24, –25.

30.

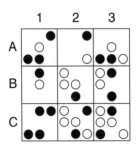

Tile 2C is incorrect and should be replaced by tile E.

Assessment

Scores between:	Rating
27–30	Very highly exceptional
24–26	High expert
21–23	Expert
19–20	Very high average
17–18	High average
13–16	Middle average
10–12	Low average
6–9	Borderline low
3–5	Low
0–2	Very low

Answers to IQ Test Nine

1. b.

2. 3 in 4. The possible combinations of drawing the balls are:

    odd – odd

    odd – even

    even – odd

    even – even

    There is only one of these combinations where an odd numbered ball is not drawn out. The chance of drawing at least one odd-numbered ball is therefore three in four.

3. unreserved

4. D: reverse the top row of numbers and add 1 to each number.

5. D: in each row across, the second square is a combination of all the lines and symbols in the other three squares.

6. D: start at the bottom left-hand corner square, then work up the first column, and back down the second etc, repeating the letters BNDKLFAGR.

7. dollar: it can be prefixed with bottom (bottom dollar). The rest can be prefixed with top (top secret, top hat, top coat, top notch).

8. 125 lb: reverse the calculations; so $48.75 \div 0.75 = 65$, $65 \div 0.8 = 81.25$ and $81.25 \div 0.65 = 125$.

9. C

10. Synonyms: unlucky, hapless
     Antonym: blessed

11.

Looking across and down, the contents of the third tile are
determined by the contents of the first two tiles. Only when
the same coloured circle appears in the same position in these
two tiles is it carried forward to the third tile; however, two
black circles change to a white circle and vice versa.

12. The *immature* flower bud *blooms* and develops into an oval
     fruit that *splits* open at maturity, revealing a mass of *long*
     white hairs that cover the numerous seeds.

13. B: the others are all in the same order albeit starting at a
     different position.

14. dell, canyon

15. 60 minutes. Total time for 8 players = 8 × 90 = 720 minutes.
     However, as 12 people (8 + 4) are on the pitch an equal length
     of time, they are each on the pitch for 60 minutes (720 ÷ 12).

16.

4	+	5	÷	3	=	3
×	■	−	■	×	■	+
6	−	4	×	2	=	4
÷	■	×	■	−	■	−
8	−	3	+	1	=	6
=	■	=	■	=	■	=
3	+	3	−	5	=	1

17. Synonyms: aromatic, redolent
    Antonym: acrid

18. B

19. Switch A is faulty.

20. a

21. B

22. E: all the others have four twigs on the left-side branch and three twigs on the right side. Option E is the other way round.

23. c, high: He worried that his business would inevitably suffer if nothing was done to relieve the burden of **high** interest rates.

24. 480: add 1 + 5 + 3 = 9. 864 ÷ 9 = 96, 96 × 5 = 480.

25. cheerful

26. 70 and 76 should be interchanged. The top sequence progresses –4, –8, –16. The bottom sequence progresses –6, –9, –12.

27. D: each pair of symbols has been swapped round.

28. rear, vanguard

29. leaf, tuber

30. 41: the sequence progresses +1, +2, +4, +8, +16, +32.

Assessment

Scores between:	Rating
27–30	Very highly exceptional
24–26	High expert
21–23	Expert
19–20	Very high average
17–18	High average
13–16	Middle average
10–12	Low average
6–9	Borderline low
3–5	Low
0–2	Very low

Answers to IQ Test Ten

1. Top row 49, middle row 7 and bottom row 56. All numbers are increasing multiples of the middle number and are in the same position in each grid, for example in the bottom left-hand corner $6 \times 3 = 18$ and $6 \times 7 = 42$.

2. equable

3. Synonyms: flagrant, blatant
    Antonym: subtle

4. 148: the sequence progresses $\times 3 + 1$ at each stage.

5. 1 foot: sapling = 1 foot, fence = 4 feet.

6. C: add the contents of the first two boxes to obtain the contents of the third box, except when two lines or symbols appear in the same position in the first two boxes, in which case they are cancelled out.

7. around, right

8. 60 and 55 should be interchanged. The top sequence progresses +7, +14, +21, +28. The bottom sequence progresses +8, +16, +24, +32.

9. The *old* city battlements, recently converted into promenades, command a *magnificent* view of the *surrounding* alpine scenery.

10. E

11. Synonyms: pseudo, spurious
    Antonym: authentic

12. 26 cm: $10^2 + 24^2 = 100 + 576 = 676$. $\sqrt{676} = 26$ (Pythagoras).

13. B

14. Switch D is faulty.

15. C

16. 11 punnets each containing 23 strawberries. 253 is the product of two prime numbers 11 and 23.

17. incidental: it is unimportant. The rest are important.

18.

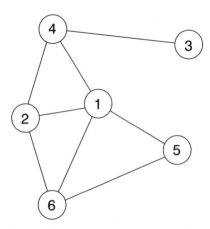

19. SKELETAL: each word commences with the middle two letters of the previous word in reverse.

20. D: only when a certain coloured dot appears in the same position once in the first three circles is it carried forward to the final circle.

21. THE LANDS = Shetland. The fish are sturgeon (so urgent), haddock (odd hack), sardine (sandier) catfish (fit cash) and flounder (unfolder).

22. c

23. idiomatic, vernacular

24. The rule is replace + − with −. −12 −15 = −27.

25. G

26. A and E

27. d, briskly: Melt a teaspoonful of butter in the pan, add the cake mixture, and stir **briskly** over a medium heat.

28. trumpet, flute

29. 28917: arrange each set of numbers so that a square number is followed by its square root, for example 32418 (√324 = 18).

30.

Assessment

Scores between:	Rating
27–30	Very highly exceptional
24–26	High expert
21–23	Expert
19–20	Very high average
17–18	High average
13–16	Middle average
10–12	Low average
6–9	Borderline low
3–5	Low
0–2	Very low

Answers to IQ Test Eleven

1. exalted

2. D: the others all contain the same 12 symbols, D contains the same symbol twice.

3. 20 buses: 665 people sit on the first 19 buses and the remainder (24) travel on the last bus.

4. ARHCLO = choral

5. b

6. C: A is the same as D with black/white reversal and similarly B is the same as E.

7. Synonyms: vague, abstruse
   Antonym: manifest

8. Switch C is faulty.

9. A: looking across letters progress –1, –2, –3 in the alphabet. Looking down they progress –3, –2, –1.

10. 6473

11. *Deselect* this *option* if you do not want to use the user name *given* here as an *e-mail* name.

12. 30: the sequence progresses –7, –14, –21, –28.

13. jackal: it is a dog, the rest are cats.

14. A: the bottom six-digit number is double the top six-digit number.

15. B: each row of three tiles across and down contains a white dot, striped dot and black dot, and a line in each of three positions.

16. C, predecessor: By adopting a more consensual leadership style than his **predecessor**, he sought to restore party unity on integration with Europe and other issues.

17.

2	×	8	–	7	=	9
+	■	+	■	–	■	–
5	–	3	×	4	=	8
–	■	–	■	×	■	×
6	–	5	+	1	=	2
=	■	=	■	=	■	=
1	×	6	÷	3	=	2

18.

Lines (both broken and unbroken) continue into adjoining tiles across and down.

19. Synonyms: abrupt, offhand

Antonym: attentive

20. 20.7 cm: $(17.55 \div 3.9) \times 4.6$.

21. pressure, force

22. 22 and 26 should be interchanged. In both sequences, add the last digit each time to obtain the next number.

23. E: each group of four circles is reversed.

24. oblique, transverse

25. D

26. D

27. 71: combined age in 15 years = 107. 4 × 15 = 60, therefore combined age now is 107 – 60 = 47. In 6 years' time, therefore, combined age will be 47 + 24 (4 × 6) = 71.

28. ethical

29. A

30. B: looking across, add a horizontal line to the right-hand pair of symbols. Looking down, add a vertical line to the bottom pair of symbols.

Assessment

Scores between:	Rating
27–30	Very highly exceptional
24–26	High expert
21–23	Expert
19–20	Very high average
17–18	High average
13–16	Middle average
10–12	Low average
6–9	Borderline low
3–5	Low
0–2	Very low

Answers to IQ Test Twelve

1. −17: the rule is replace − + with −. −4 −13 = −17.

2. speed, increase

3. E

4. C and D

5. confident

6. D: lines are carried forward from the first two squares to the third square, except when two lines appear in the same position in the first two squares, in which case they are cancelled out.

7. 25, 29. There are two alternate sequences: start at 10 and add 3, 5, 7; start at 50 and deduct 5, 7, 9.

8. D

9. Switch C is faulty.

10. 29: (31 + 2) − 29 = 4.

11. D. economic: Cuttlefish have some **economic** importance, not only for their flesh, which is eaten in many countries, but also for the bone of their shell and for the ink they eject to cloud the water as protection from their enemies.

12. parameter, criterion

13.

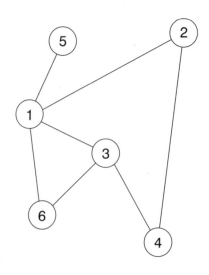

14. D: Each line, both across and down, contains one of the four different symbols.

15. Synonyms: blithe, buoyant
    Antonym: morose

16. D

17. Synonyms: inanimate, inert
    Antonym: active

18. 15 and 11: 1 + 2 + 3 + 4 = 10, then insert next two numbers 11, 12 and add digits 1 + 1 + 1 + 2 = 5. Insert next two numbers 6, 7 and add digits 6 + 7 = 13. Insert next two numbers 14, 15 and add digits 1 + 4 + 1 + 5 = **11**.

19. hem: combine the first four words with the second four words, to produce mayhem, ridden, barrow, sealed.

20. 4600: (552 ÷ 12) × 100.

21. The *common* peafowl has been *domesticated* in many parts of the *world* but there are *feral* populations in some *Pacific* islands.

22. B

23. Danube, Euphrates, Volga

24. torpid: it means sluggish or lacking energy. The rest mean careless or slack.

25. 6.75 and 7.5 should be interchanged. The top sequence progresses + 2.25 at each stage. The bottom sequence progresses + 2.75 at each stage

26. C: Working clockwise the dots swap places two at a time, starting with the black circle and the circle with the dot.

27. C: looking across, lines progress +2, –3, +2. Looking down, columns progress +3, –2, +3.

28. circle, column: a pie chart consists of a circle and a bar chart consists of columns.

29. 18: in each column add the first two numbers, then divide the sum by 3 to obtain the bottom number, ie (4 + 11) ÷ 3 = 5.

30.

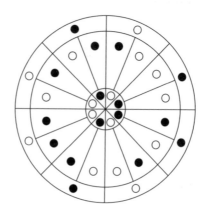

In the three rings of dots, a white dot is always opposite a black dot and vice versa.

Assessment

Scores between:	Rating
27–30	Very highly exceptional
24–26	High expert
21–23	Expert
19–20	Very high average
17–18	High average
13–16	Middle average
10–12	Low average
6–9	Borderline low
3–5	Low
0–2	Very low

Overall assessment for all twelve tests

320–360	Very highly exceptional
290–319	High expert
250–289	Expert
230–249	Very high average
200–229	High average
160–199	Middle average
120–159	Low average
70–119	Borderline low
30–69	Low
0–29	Very low

Analysis

In addition to the above general performance rating, it is recommended that you analyse your performance for each of the different types of questions, and in particular for verbal aptitude, numerical aptitude and spatial aptitude questions. An analysis of your performance in each of these categories will enable you to build and capitalise on your strengths, and work on improving performance in areas of weakness.

Verbal aptitude

Verbal intelligence is a measurement of your capacity to use language in order to express yourself, comprehend written text and understand other people. People who possess a high level of verbal skills often excel in fields such as writing (author, journalist, editor, critic), teaching (language, drama), legal profession (judge/barrister/lawyer), personnel work (advocate, human resources, counsellor) and as actors, psychologists, interpreters and interviewers.

Numerical aptitude

We all require some numerical skills in our lives, whether it is to calculate our weekly shopping bill or to budget how to use our monthly income. Mathematical intelligence tests generally explore your ability to reason and to perform basic arithmetic functions. Good mathematical ability is an excellent stepping stone to career success in jobs such as accounting or banking. People who possess a high level of numerical skills also often excel in jobs such as auditor, business consultant, financial analyst, mathematics or science teacher, quantity surveyor, tax adviser, company secretary, computer programmer or stockbroker.

Spatial aptitude

The ability being investigated in questions of spatial aptitude is how well a person is able to identify patterns and meaning from what might appear at first glance random or very complex information. This type of abstract reasoning does not involve problems that are verbal or numerical in nature. As spatial aptitude involves quite different thought processes from those that determine verbal or numerical aptitude, it is quite common for people who score very highly on numerical and verbal aptitude tests to score equally badly on spatial aptitude tests and vice versa.

This is because the left side of the human brain is analytical and functions in a sequential and logical fashion, and is the side that controls language, academic studies and rationality. The right side of the brain is creative and intuitive and leads, for example, to the birth of ideas for works of art and music. It is the side of the brain that determines how well we are able to adapt to tests of spatial aptitude. As many people have some degree of brain bias, they thus perform better on tests that involve thought processes controlled by the stronger side of their brain.

People who scored badly on spatial aptitude questions, after performing well on verbal and numerical aptitude questions, should therefore have no great cause for concern. They have, however, the opportunity to practise and increase their performance on this type of spatial aptitude testing and to develop their right-brain thinking.

People who possess a high level of spatial aptitude often excel in fields such as architecture, photography, engineering design, decorating, and as artists, carpenters, landscape designers, cartoon animators, guides, fashion designers, shop fitters and civil engineers.

ALSO AVAILABLE FROM KOGAN PAGE

ISBN: 978 0 7494 4969 8
Paperback 2008

ISBN: 978 0 7494 5229 2
Paperback 2008

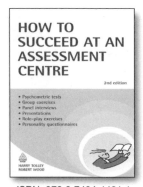

ISBN: 978 0 7494 4421 1
Paperback 2005

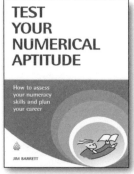

ISBN: 978 0 7494 5064 9
Paperback 2007

Buy online at:
www.koganpage.com

ALSO AVAILABLE FROM KOGAN PAGE

ISBN-13: 978 0 7494 5106 6
Paperback 2007

ISBN: 978 0 7494 4852 3
Paperback 2007

ISBN: 978 0 7494 4954 4
Paperback 2007

ISBN: 978 0 7494 5165 3
Paperback 2008

Buy online at:
www.koganpage.com

ALSO AVAILABLE FROM KOGAN PAGE

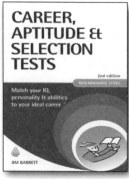

ISBN: 978 0 7494 4819 6
Paperback 2006

ISBN: 978 0 7494 4931 5
Paperback 2007

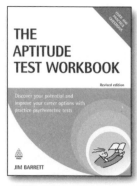

ISBN: 978 0 7494 5237 7
Paperback 2008

ISBN: 978 0 7494 3887 6
Paperback 2003

Buy online at:
www.koganpage.com

ALSO AVAILABLE FROM KOGAN PAGE

ISBN: 978 0 7494 4946 9
Paperback 2007

ISBN: 978 0 7494 4853 0
Paperback 2007

ISBN: 978 0 7494 4274 3
Paperback 2004

ISBN: 978 0 7494 5161 5
Paperback 2008

Buy online at:
www.koganpage.com